Keeping and Breeding Lizards

Their Natural History
and Care in Captivity

Chris Mattison

BLANDFORD

A BLANDFORD BOOK

First published in paperback in the UK 1996 by Blandford
A Cassell Imprint

CASSELL PLC
Wellington House
125 Strand
London WC2R 0BB

Previously published in hardback 1991

Distributed in the United States by
Sterling Publishing Co., Inc.
387 Park Avenue South, New York, NY 10016-8810

Distributed in Australia by
Capricorn Link (Australia) Pty Ltd
PO Box 665, Lane Cove, NSW 2066

British Library Cataloguing in Publication Data
Mattison, Christopher
  Keeping and breeding lizards.
  I. Pets: Lizards. Breeding & care
  I. Title
  639.395
ISBN 0-7137-2632-6

Typeset by Litho Link Ltd, Welshpool, Powys, Wales

Printed and bound in Hong Kong by Dah Hua

Contents

Acknowledgements   7

Editorial Note   8

Introduction   9

Chapter 1   Essential Biology:
            What Every Lizard-keeper Should Know   13

Chapter 2   Cages: A Home Away From Home   17

Chapter 3   Heating, Lighting and Humidity:
            Getting the Environment Right   21

Chapter 4   Outdoor Enclosures: 'Al Fresco' Lizards   27

Chapter 5   Natural Vivaria   32

Chapter 6   Food and Feeding: the Menu   42

Chapter 7   Breeding   52

Chapter 8   Health and Management: Staying in Shape   60

Chapter 9   The Eublepharid 'Geckos'   69

Chapter 10 Geckos   79

Chapter 11 Snake Lizards   110

Chapter 12 Night Lizards   112

Chapter 13 Iguanas   114

Chapter 14 Agamids   138

Chapter 15 Skinks   154

Chapter 16 Lacertids: Wall Lizards and Related Species   171

Chapter 17   Tegus, Ameivas and Racerunners   181

Chapter 18   Alligator Lizards, Legless Lizards and Galliwasps   185

Chapter 19   Girdle-tailed Lizards, Plated Lizards
             and Related Species   191

Chapter 20   Chameleons   197

Chapter 21   The Chinese Crocodile Lizard   203

Chapter 22   The Gila Monster and Beaded Lizard   205

Chapter 23   Monitors   211

Chapter 24   Amphisbaenians: Worm Lizards   214

             Societies, Journals and Magazines   217

             Bibliography   219

             Index   220

6

Acknowledgements

Once again, I am indebted to many people who helped out with the loan of specimens, answered questions or assisted in other ways.

Photographs were taken with the help and co-operation of the following persons and institutions:

Bob Applegate; Harry Baird; David Baker; Gretchen Davison; Jeremy Fletcher; Gareth Griffiths, Manchester Pets and Aquatics; Lee Grismer; Victor C. Kuilenburg, Dierenpark Ouwehand, Rhenen, Holland; Bob Mailloux; Bill Montgomery; James Murphy, Dallas Zoo; Mike Nolan; Jeffrey Nunan; Sue Patterson, Locusta; John Pickett; Paul Rowley and Keith Brown, Chester Zoo; Terry Thatcher; Phillipe de Vosjoli.

Dave Garthwaite supplied a paper on New Zealand geckos of which I was unaware and Jeffrey Nunan generously supplied a copy of his paper on the care of diplodactyline geckos before it had appeared in print.

To all these people, and to many others who helped in less specific areas, I extend my thanks and appreciation.

Editorial Note

METRIC CONVERSIONS

Throughout this book all measurements of temperature and length are given as metric.

Those readers who are more familiar with the Fahrenheit thermometer or the Imperial System of measurement might find the following formulae and conversion tables useful.

Temperature

To convert °C to °F:
× 9 ÷ 5 + 32

°C		°F
10	=	50
15	=	59
20	=	68
25	=	77
30	=	86
35	=	95
40	=	104
45	=	113
50	=	122

Length

To convert cm to in:
÷ 2.54

cm		in.	
1	=	0.39	
5	=	1.97	
10	=	3.94	
15	=	5.91	
20	=	7.87	
25	=	9.84	
30	=	11.81	
35	=	13.78	
40	=	15.75	
50	=	19.66	
60	=	23.62	
75	=	29.53	
100 (1 m)	=	39.37	(3.3 ft)
200 (2 m)	=	78.74	(6.6 ft)
400 (4 m)	=	157.48	(13.1 ft)

Introduction

Of all the reptiles, lizards are the most colourful and lively. It is only natural, then, that they compete with tropical birds and fish for the attention of wild animal keepers. Many of the smaller species can be housed in semi-natural 'landscaped' vivariums, along with a selection of attractive plants. For this reason, a brief introduction to the fascinating aspect of creating natural set-ups has been included, together with some elementary advice on the choice of suitable plants and their culture.

Unfortunately, brightly coloured lizards, newly imported from their natural environments, frequently fade, both in colour and in health, when confined to a cage. This leads to a disenchantment with them and with reptile-keeping in general. In order to avoid this situation, a number of basic biological facts must be learned before lizards can be kept successfully and humanely. The object of this book is not to encourage the keeping of lizards in captivity *per se* but to attempt to improve the conditions under which they are kept and to promote the cause of captive breeding.

In an evolutionary context, lizards are the most successful reptiles, both in terms of numbers of species and numbers of individuals. This is due, at least in part, to their great diversity, acquired through the processes of natural selection. The driving force behind this diversity has been the need to adapt to a variety of conditions in order to avoid competition with other reptiles and, more recently in geological time, birds and mammals. In addition, new types have evolved as new possibilities in terms of food and habitat have arisen due to the gradually changing global environment. Thus we find lizards distributed from the Arctic Circle in the north to Tierra del Fuego in the south, from the tree-tops to the sub-soil layers and from the most arid parts of the world to almost totally aquatic habitats.

Furthermore, and unlike snake-keeping, for instance, lizard-keeping has not polarised towards one or two particular groups of species, or to species from a particular region. Temperate and tropical species, terrestrial, arboreal and aquatic species, nocturnal and diurnal species and herbivorous and carnivorous species are all grist to the mill of some enthusiast somewhere. Indeed, lizards encompassing several of these categories are often kept in a single collection. It follows from this that, in order to keep alive a varied selection of lizard species, a whole range of conditions will be needed, taking into account the specialisations and adaptations of the species concerned. There is therefore no set formula for keeping and breeding lizards, or even for obtaining a starting point from which modifications and improvisations can be made for the odd atypical species: all must be considered individually or in small groups of species having similar requirements.

For this reason, the first eight chapters of this book deal mainly with general topics. It would be misleading to generalise too much about the care and breeding of so diverse a group of animals and these chapters are necessarily short. More specific information can be found in Chapters 9–24, which deal separately with the different lizard species that are suitable for keeping. Because of the large number of species which could, potentially, fall into the hands of the pet trade, and therefore the lizard-keeper, no attempt has been made to give equal attention to all species. Rather, those species most likely to be met with are described in some detail, while others which are rarely offered are mentioned only briefly or not at all. No apology is made for dwelling at some length on the species which adapt well to captivity and are willing breeders, for these are the species which should be selected, especially by beginners. As more experience is gained, then other, more difficult species can be attempted: by this time enough background knowledge and a 'feel' for lizard-keeping will have developed and detailed advice will not be so essential. It is hoped that the care of those species not included can be deduced by cautious extrapolation of the advice given for similar or related species and by using techniques such as temperature and humidity gradients in order to ensure that conditions within the cage or enclosure are varied enough for the lizard to be in the right place at the right time.

Although the species are listed under their families it should be obvious that the various species within each family may require totally different environments and that, conversely, species from different families may have similar requirements. For example, desert lizards from various parts of the world have several requirements in common with each other which transcend any taxonomic affinities. For this reason, some large families have been split up into groups of species which need roughly similar conditions and there will be some cross-referencing to groups of species in other families if these have similar requirements.

The best method of using this book will be to follow the hierarchical arrangement in which it is written; information given under the species accounts is supplementary to the notes given at the beginning of each section, where applicable, and these in turn are supplementary to the introductions to each family. Where the species in question is not listed, information given for similar or related species should be studied. In order to avoid repetition throughout, it has been assumed that the general chapters have been read first.

CHAPTER 1

Essential Biology:
What Every Lizard-keeper
Should Know

Because lizards differ radically from other animals which the reader may have kept in captivity, it is important to be aware of three or four important aspects of their biology which have a direct bearing on their maintenance and breeding. These are: the way in which they regulate their body temperature; their social systems and, in particular, their territorial behaviour; the way in which they metabolise calcium; and the way in which the sex of offspring is determined in some species.

THERMOREGULATION

Firstly, lizards are reptiles and, as such, they are ectothermic. In other words, they rely on outside sources of heat to keep their body temperatures at the level at which they function best. The preferred temperature varies from species to species, but is generally between 25°C and 35°C, although it may be higher, exceptionally up to 40°C for a few desert species. Species' preferred temperatures, however, do not always reflect the climate in the part of the world from which they come. Most active, diurnal species, for instance, have similar preferred temperatures whether they come from Madagascar or Manchester; those from cooler climates just spend more time and effort keeping their temperatures topped-up. Temperature is regulated by moving from cool to warm micro-environments and back again, according to the conditions, and some species increase the rate at which they raise their body temperature by having dark coloration, by basking in open sunlight (often orientating their bodies at a right angle to the direction of the sun) or by flattening their bodies against rocks and sand, etc. which have been heated by the sun. By these means, they are capable of maintaining very accurate control of their body temperatures – within a fraction of a degree where necessary. Other species, such as those living beneath the ground, have less opportunity for active thermoregulation and, for this reason, are often restricted to warmer parts of the world or have adapted to a lower 'operating temperature'.

If a species' body temperature falls much below that which it prefers, it will attempt to raise it by one of the methods listed above, or it will seek shelter. If it allows its body temperature to fall too low it will become sluggish and may eventually lose the power of locomotion altogether; it needs to be in a secure hiding place if this is likely to happen. Similarly, if it becomes too hot, its activity will be impaired and it will eventually die of heat exhaustion. The upper and lower limits vary according to the species and to the temperature range they are likely to experience within their natural environment. Tropical species are less tolerant of cold conditions than are those from northern Europe, for instance, whereas desert species are better adapted to extremely high temperatures. In those parts of the world where a cold winter is experienced, the lizard species will have evolved a pattern of annual hibernation in order to avoid lethally cold temperatures, while some desert species may become less active at the height of summer in order to avoid lethally high temperatures (also in some cases to avoid drought).

There is a further complication. It has been shown that, in some species at least, different temperatures are necessary at different times of the year, and sometimes at different times of the day, for certain physiological processes to take place. For instance, male *Anolis* lizards which are kept constantly at their 'preferred' temperature range fail to develop viable sperm and often die sooner than individuals given a seasonal temperature fluctuation. Similarly, if wall lizards (*Podarcis* species) are given a choice of temperatures in a cage with a heater at one end, they will voluntarily seek out cooler areas during the night.

All of these factors must be taken into account when creating the environment for captive lizards and, although it is not feasible to know precisely what temperature a particular lizard requires every minute of the day and every month of the year, it is pretty safe to assume that the lizard itself will know. The obvious solution, then, is to provide a choice of temperatures in different parts of the cage and leave the rest to the lizard. Suitable methods of doing this, and advice on the equipment required, are given in Chapter 3.

TERRITORIALITY

A second essential biological factor which must be taken into account is territoriality. Unlike most snakes, for example, lizards are often highly territorial. In most cases it is the males which demand exclusive rights to a piece of territory (and the females living in it), but females can also be territorial. Conflict is most likely to arise during the breeding season, but under the artificial conditions imposed by the close confinement of captivity it is often necessary to keep males, and sometimes females, separated all the time once they are sexually mature.

Territoriality is expressed by displays between individuals and may culminate in fighting. Eventually, a dominance hierarchy is attained, with one male animal dominant over one or more subordinate males. In nature, these subordinate animals would seek new territories but in a cage there is rarely enough space for this to occur and, even if they are not subjected to physical violence, they will be placed under severe stress, often refuse to feed and eventually die. This situation must obviously be avoided and, in order to do so, it is essential to be able to distinguish males from females. Where this is not possible, e.g. in some skinks and most monitors, overspill accommodation must be made available so that animals can be segregated should fighting occur.

VITAMIN D METABOLISM

The third essential piece of biology to understand is concerned with lizards' metabolism, especially with regard to vitamin D, calcium and phosphorus. Certain species, especially the more colourful ones, are unable to obtain vitamin D from their food through the normal digestive processes. Instead, they rely on the ultra-violet which is present in sunlight to react with specialised cells near the surface of their skin, to produce this essential vitamin. Vitamin D3 is important in calcium and phosphorus assimilation and without it bones become de-calcified, leading to a ricket-like condition. It is important to note that this occurs even if additional calcium and phosphorus are given with the food, because without the vitamin D3 they cannot be used by the body.

There are two schools of thought as to how best to overcome the problem, and both are probably effective if carried out carefully. Most simply, the required amount of vitamin D3 can be added to the food along with extra calcium (most diets will contain plenty of phosphorus and this can be left to look after itself). Alternatively, a source of ultra-violet, in the form of a special lamp, can be provided to simulate that which is in sunlight, thereby allowing the lizards to produce their own vitamin D3 in a more natural manner. An added complication is that the varied diets of wild lizards are all but impossible to match in

15

captivity and so dietary supplements are often necessary anyway. This can confuse the issue somewhat and makes the results obtained from either method difficult to assess. These problems, and some of the ways around them, are discussed more fully in Chapter 3.

TEMPERATURE DEPENDENT SEX DETERMINATION

Most animals with which the reader will be familiar have the sex of their offspring determined at the moment of fertilisation. This is known as genetic sex determination and applies to some species of lizard. Other species, however, use a method known as temperature dependent sex determination (TDSD) in which the sex of the offspring is not fixed at the time of fertilisation, nor even when the egg is laid, but changes during incubation according to the temperature. It appears that there is a 'time window', usually during the early part of incubation, when the sex can swing one way or the other. If, at this time, the eggs are cooler than a certain critical temperature the young will be female and if they are warmer they will be male. The critical temperature probably varies from species to species but will usually be around 30°C. The implications of this phenomenon are that if all the eggs from a certain species are incubated at the same temperature, then only one sex will be produced (this was how TDSD was first discovered in lizards). On the other hand, provided the critical temperature is known, the informed breeder has the distinct advantage of being able to produce only that sex which is required, or a fixed ratio between the sexes, usually a predominance of females.

All of the species of eublepharids and geckos which have so far been investigated show TDSD, as have some species in other families. It seems probable that TDSD is fairly widespread amongst lizards, at least in the more 'primitive' families, i.e. those which evolved early on. When breeding species for which there is no information, good records should be kept of the incubation temperature and the eventual sexes of the hatchlings. If a pattern does emerge, this information can be used to manipulate the sex ratio of further clutches of eggs, and should be published so that other breeders can also be aware of the situation.

CHAPTER 2

Cages: A Home Away From Home

With very few exceptions, most lizard-keepers will need to buy, build or adapt a cage in which to keep their animals. Because of the huge diversity in size, to say nothing of varying habits and activity patterns, there is no one design which is even remotely versatile enough for all the species which might potentially end up in a collection. It is necessary, therefore, to consider very carefully the requirements of the species in question before suitable accommodation can be provided.

All other things being equal, large lizards require bigger cages than small ones. Unfortunately, all other things rarely *are* equal, and it is sometimes necessary to provide more space for a group of small, highly active lizards, for instance, than for one large sluggish individual. Other factors which have to be taken into account are: the necessity or otherwise of incorporating separate lighting and/or heating inside the cage; whether the lizards need to climb or burrow; how many are to be kept together; whether the cage is to be put on display in, say, a living room, and if it is to contain living plants. If the species is unable to climb smooth surfaces, it may not be necessary to build a lid for the cage, unless it feeds on creatures such as crickets and flies, or unless there is a danger of other household pets, or children, climbing in and terrifying or eating the inhabitants!

Starting with the smallest type of cage possible, small plastic lunch-boxes are useful for rearing juvenile lizards of the smaller species, especially if large numbers of these need to be accommodated separately. Of course, it is not possible to provide heating for each individual container and so the boxes must be kept in a warm room or placed on a suitable source of heat such as a heat strip or heat pad. Several designs of base heaters are readily available in Europe and North America. These should be placed towards the back of the shelf on which the boxes rest, so that heat is applied at one end only, giving the lizard a choice of temperatures and, if necessary, a thermostat

17

1.   Very small or young lizards can be kept most simply in a small plastic box, heated at one end and provided with a suitable substrate, a water bowl and somewhere to hide.

should be included in the circuit to prevent the cage from overheating – the temperature at the cool end should not go above about 21–23°C at any time, irrespective of the species in the box. Similarly, lighting equipment, where necessary, must be placed outside the box and this can conveniently be achieved by suspending a fluorescent tube above the shelf on which the boxes are placed. Each box should be furnished with a piece of kitchen tissue or a layer of sand or grit. A small water bowl should be placed at the end furthest from the heat source, and a small segment of bark or stone will provide somewhere for the lizard to hide. Because of the space limitations in such containers, they are only suitable for small, inactive species such as terrestrial geckos.

A small aquarium can be pressed into use for slightly larger species. Depending on its size, it will accommodate one, or a pair, of small lizards such as the wall lizards, medium sized geckos or skinks, and juveniles of some of the larger species. Very active lizards, especially of the more nervous kinds, may damage themselves by running headlong into the glass whenever they are disturbed and it may be beneficial to paint this or to line it with bark or rockwork. Again, heat should be applied to one end and it should be possible to make use of a spotlight, allowing one to keep some of the basking species in this type of container. If a lid is required, to confine either the lizards or their meals, this can be constructed from wood, and should incorporate

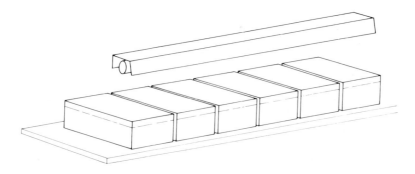

Fig. 1. Small plastic boxes arranged on a shelf, showing a method of providing ultra-violet light to the occupants.

plenty of mesh panels for ventilation. It is sometimes possible to purchase vivarium lids, designed to fit the standard sizes of aquaria, and already fitted with ventilation and a light-holder.

Rather than use a purchased aquarium, which will have been designed for fish, it may be better to design and build a glass cage specifically for the lizards, using silicone aquarium sealant as an adhesive. In this way, account can be taken of the lizards' habits and preferences, so the cage could be tall for climbing species, shallow for terrestrial or burrowing species or divided into land and water areas for semi-aquatic species. All-glass cages are not difficult to make if the glass is bought already cut to size, and instructions can be found in any of the aquarium books or magazines. Lizard-keepers with fertile imaginations can develop this idea further by building in features such as running water with a hidden compartment for the pumps and filters, niches for planting epiphytic plants and even oddly shaped cages to fit oddly shaped corners, but the lizards' welfare is of paramount importance and their requirements should not be compromised by way-out designs.

Moving up a size, larger lizards, and those species requiring large territories, will need specially constructed enclosures. These are most commonly made of wood, with a glass front for viewing. The panes of glass can be made to slide to one side in order to offer food to the inmates and for cleaning and so on, or access may be obtained through the top. Again, it may or may not be necessary to build a lid for the cage, although uncoated timber is more easily climbed than glass – plastic-faced composition board (e.g. Conti-board in Europe) is the best choice of material. Where the cage is to contain a damp substrate, or where regular spraying is necessary, timber is not a good choice,

19

however, unless it can be thoroughly sealed, with an epoxy resin, for instance.

All the above suggestions can be scaled up or down according to the requirements and size of the lizards or the number to be housed. However, the cage merely acts as a container for the lizards, and further thought must go into creating a suitable environment for them.

CHAPTER 3

Heating, Lighting and Humidity: Getting the Environment Right

The physical factors affecting the health and happiness of all animals can be broken down into three main elements: heat, light and humidity. Lizards differ in the amounts of each of these required, and the provision of a suitable range of these variables is accomplished by the sensible use of various items of equipment.

HEATING

Lizard cages can be heated by means of radiant heat or conducted heat, or by a combination of both. Equipment designed to provide radiant heat consists of light-bulbs, spotlights, ceramic heaters or tubular heaters. Light-bulbs and spotlights provide light as well as heat, but this can sometimes be a disadvantage. Species which bask in the wild are conditioned to move in and out of sunlight and to acquire heat more or less directly from the sun. These species, then, should be provided with an overhead heat-source, together with a light. The light need not be integral with the heater, however, and it is probably better to install a separate fluorescent light in such a way that when the lizard basks in the heat it is also exposed to light (see below, under Lighting). The most important thing is that the heat-source is positioned at one end of the cage. This will create a thermal gradient, allowing the lizards to move backwards and forwards, just as they would in the wild. Temperatures beneath the heater are then not so critical – if the lizards find this site too hot they will move away. Therefore, a fairly high temperature directly beneath the heater should be aimed at – up to 50°C for desert species. This area is known as the 'hot-spot'. Elsewhere in the cage the lizards can move about, finding areas of varying temperature and so regulate their body temperature by choosing where to be at any given time.

In order for the heating arrangements to be as natural as possible for

21

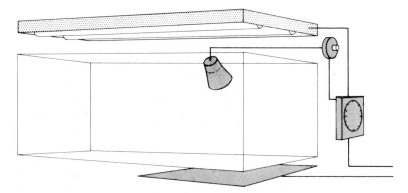

Fig. 2. A suggested arrangement for providing heating and lighting for basking species. The lights and spotlight are wired through a time switch: the spotlight may also be controlled by a thermostat to prevent overheating if necessary. The heat pad is permanently switched on in order to provide background heating.

basking species, the temperature should be allowed to fall during the night – the actual values for day and night temperatures will vary with the species, but the general pattern will always be the same. The best way of arranging for this is to install an automatic time switch between the overhead heater and the electricity supply. If, when the heater is switched off, the temperature is likely to fall to near lethal limits for the species, then another, secondary, means of heating will be needed. The best way of doing this is through conducted heat, and this should be kept at a low level, giving a steady, gentle, background heat, that can be left on during the day and night.

Conducted heat is best applied to the floor of the cage by a heating element placed underneath. The element itself can be a heating strip or tape, or a heating mat. Again, the heat should be applied to one section only of the cage floor, giving the lizards ample opportunity to maintain their preferred body temperature day and night.

For non-basking and burrowing species, provide only an underfloor heat-source as described above. In all cases, give the lizards a choice of temperatures at all times by applying heat to one area, about one-quarter to one half, of the cage.

LIGHTING

Lighting is an important factor in lizard-keeping for a number of reasons.

Species which bask probably have a psychological need to be exposed to bright light for at least part of each day, thus satisfying their

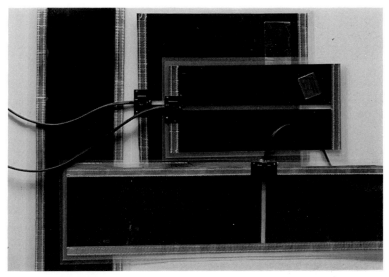

2.   Thin heat-strips or pads are ideal for providing background heating: they should be arranged so that only one end of the cage is heated.

natural tendency to bask in bright sunshine. In addition, all species except those which live near the equator will experience a seasonal pattern of long and short days. These seasonal changes are important in bringing the lizards into breeding condition. As far as is known, all lizards in which seasonal breeding occurs become sexually active in response to lengthening days (i.e. in the spring). In some cases, mating takes place only at this time and a single clutch of eggs or young is produced later in the summer, but in other species once breeding activity begins it continues throughout the warmer months (and longer days) and several clutches may be produced. For these reasons, not only must a suitable means of lighting be provided, but attention must be paid to photoperiod. Although many captive lizards will respond to the natural photoperiod if they are housed in a room with windows, others can be stimulated more effectively by altering the day/night cycle gradually throughout the year. As a rule of thumb, sixteen hours of light should be given at the height of summer and eight in the middle of winter. The seasons can, theoretically, be shifted by manipulating the light cycle, so that the lizards are in breeding condition when it is winter outside but, in practice, daylight entering through windows tends to confuse the issue (and, presumably, the lizards) and so it is best to vary the lighting in keeping with local conditions. Some trouble may be experienced with southern

23

hemisphere species kept in the northern hemisphere, and *vice versa*. Often, the in-built biological rythms of these species are not easily altered by manipulation of the light regime and their breeding seasons will be the reverse of local species. Once they have bred in captivity, however, their offspring will usually fit into the local pattern.

A secondary, but equally important, function of lighting is to provide vitamin D3 to certain species of lizards. Most of the lizards which bask obtain a large proportion of their vitamin D3 from the ultra-violet rays in sunlight. Vitamin D3 is essential for the assimilation of calcium, and without it the bones become deformed and various other defects occur. Unfortunately, incandescent light-bulbs and the majority of fluorescent tubes do not produce ultra-violet in any appreciable quantity and are therefore useless for vitamin D3 synthesis. For those species which need ultra-violet, special tubes are available. These range from tubes which simulate natural sunlight in its entire range of wavelengths, including some ultra-violet, to tubes which emit almost exclusively ultra-violet. It is important to note that ultra-violet radiation is classified into two types according to the wavelengths involved, ultra-violet A and ultra-violet B. Ultra-violet B is the most effective for vitamin D3 formation but, unfortunately, radiation of this type (wavelengths of 315–400nm) can be harmful, both to lizards and to humans, and light sources in which these wavelengths predominate should be avoided. The specifications of a selection of suitable tubes is summarised below:

TRULITE AND VITA-LITE

Trulite (in Europe) and Vita-lite (in North America) were the first fluorescent tubes to be tried out by reptile-keepers and the results were a dramatic improvement over previous arrangements. Their ultra-violet emission falls off quite early on in their life, however, and continual replacement is expensive. They provide less ultra-violet than either of the two following products and are only effective if the lizards can get very close to, or in contact with, them.

GEC BLACKLIGHT

These tubes emit ultra-violet radiation but almost no other wavelengths. They are by far the most effective way of promoting vitamin D3 formation, but they produce an eerie pale blue glow and are not suitable for use on their own. They should be fitted alongside a tube emitting a more natural spectrum of light.

ACTINIC 09

These tubes produce a natural spectrum of visible light as well as a reasonable amount of ultra-violet radiation. The overall effect is rather a 'cold' bluish light and, although lizards will bask in their rays, they are also best fitted alongside a tube giving a warmer spectrum.

Positioning of the light is just as important as its choice. It has been found that unless the lizards can get very close to the tubes they gain very little benefit. Indeed, agile species will often climb on to the tube and lie along it for hours on end with no apparent harmful effects. Obviously, species which do not climb are unable to do this and it is then necessary to mount the tube in such a way that the lizards can approach it closely. Every lizard in the cage should be able to bask within 30 cm of the tube.

In order to make any of these tubes more pleasant to look at, they should be paired up with either a normal household fluorescent tube, e.g. 'warm white', or with one of the colour-enhancing tubes such as those used by aquarium fanciers. If living plants are included in the cage, a bright, natural spectrum light-source, or a warm light containing plenty of light in the red and blue parts of the spectrum is essential. Advice on suitable plant lights is readily available from horticultural specialists.

HUMIDITY

Humidity is a function of temperature, ventilation and the amount of water contained in the cage. If a warm cage is sprayed frequently, and very little ventilation is provided, the air will soon become saturated, i.e. the humidity will be 100 per cent. At the other extreme, an open or well-ventilated cage which is never sprayed and contains little or no standing water will have a very low humidity. Different species of lizards have different preferences regarding humidity, and a knowledge of their natural history is very useful in arriving at a satisfactory condition. Unfortunately, knowing where an animal comes from is not always enough. A species from South American may occur in the soggy environment of Amazonia, the arid wastelands of the Atacama desert or the rarified atmosphere of the Andes. If the species is one which has been extensively kept and bred in captivity then it will be possible to obtain the appropriate information very easily. Otherwise, a certain amount of experimentation may be necessary.

Species which need a high degree of humidity should be sprayed regularly, preferably twice each day. Many of these species will not drink from a water bowl, relying instead on the droplets of water which collect on foliage, the sides of their cage or themselves. A high humidity requirement is not an excuse for a stagnant and unhealthy atmosphere inside the cage. Ventilation must be adequate, even if this necessitates more frequent spraying. One way around this problem is to provide running water, which will automatically raise the humidity in parts of the cage. Methods of arranging this are given later on, in the section on 'natural vivaria'.

To summarise, the interplay of three factors, heat, light and humidity, is an important aspect of lizard husbandry. Each can be varied using specialised equipment, but the key to providing successfully the right amount of each is to give the lizard(s) a choice.

CHAPTER 4

Outdoor Enclosures: 'Al Fresco' Lizards

GENERAL CONSTRUCTION

Depending on the prevailing climatic conditions, it may be possible to keep a colony of lizards outdoors in a purpose-built enclosure. This has the advantage of giving the animals much more room than can normally be provided in an indoor cage, the opportunity to behave more naturally, some access to wild food which may blunder into the enclosure and, perhaps most importantly, access to sunlight. There are limitations, however, the most obvious of which is climate. Only species which are adapted to the local climatic conditions will thrive outdoors. This limits the choice of species to those which occur naturally in your area or in areas in other parts of the world that have a similar climate. Having said this, there are a number of techniques that can be used to 'improve' on the local climate and this will widen the choice slightly.

By sloping the enclosure towards the south if you live in the northern hemisphere (or to the north in the southern hemisphere), the amount of sunlight can be maximised. Further protection can be given by building a bank of soil against the northerly wall of the enclosure. A removable glass cover can be installed and this will raise the temperature inside considerably, although it must be removed at every opportunity in order to allow ultra-violet rays to get to the lizards' basking sites and to prevent overheating. The best arrangement is to remove the glass in late spring and leave it off for the whole of the summer; at other times it can be removed during warm days but replaced at night.

Construction of the enclosure is basically the same as building a south-facing rockery, but with a wall around. A small pool should be included and, if it is hoped that the lizards will breed, and they are oviparous species, there should be an exposed area of sand, or sandy

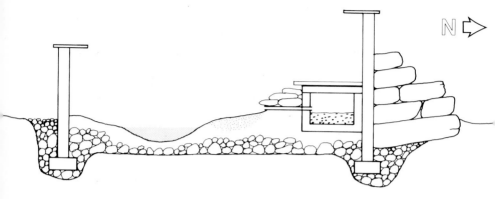

Fig. 3.   Elevation of a straightforward outdoor enclosure with a small pool and hibernaculum and areas for basking, egg-laying and so on.

soil, for egg-laying. The rockwork should be built in such a way that there are holes and crevices for the lizards to hide in, as well as open areas for basking. The whole area should be well-drained and the pool should consist of a separate construction, most conveniently built by using a rubber pool liner.

The walls of the enclosure may be of glass, concrete or timber, but brickwork or concrete blocks are probably the most versatile materials. If burrowing species are to be included, deep foundations should be dug and filled with concrete, and this will also be necessary if wild rodents, especially rats, are likely to breach the walls of the enclosure as these will wipe out a lizard colony in no time. Most importantly, netting must be placed over the entire enclosure in order to prevent predators, of which domestic cats are the main problem, from getting in. (People who live in a climate where Gila monsters, monitors, etc. can be kept outside may disregard the last piece of advice as rodents and other pests will form a useful additional food supply.) An overhang will probably be necessary to prevent the lizards from climbing out, and this can be made from smooth tiles or strips of glass cemented to the top of the walls.

Plants will be an attractive addition to the enclosure as well as providing shelter and hiding places for the lizards. Low, cushion or clump-forming species are best and, although the choice of species will depend on location, plants sold for rockeries will usually be suitable since they are slow-growing and well-suited to the dry, stony conditions. More advice on this matter is given below.

If the lizards are to be left outdoors over the winter (and it will be difficult to do otherwise if the enclosure contains plenty of hiding places), provision should be made for a hibernaculum. This consists of an insulated chamber which will remain dry and frost-free throughout the winter and into which the lizards can easily find their way. It can be filled with chopped straw, bracken or an artificial material such as vermiculite, the coarsest grade being preferred. It should not be buried below the level of the surrounding ground if there is likely to be a danger of flooding, and any tubes, etc. which give access to it should slope upwards for the same reason. It is useful if the inside of the chamber can be inspected from time to time in order to check on the welfare of any hibernating lizards and to replace any bedding. In practice, such a chamber is normally constructed at or slightly above the level of surrounding ground, with access tubes opening out at the lowest level(s) of the vivarium. It is insulated by covering it with a mound of soil and rocks with one large rock covering an inspection plate. During very cold weather it can be useful to cover the hibernaculum (or the whole enclosure if feasible) with additional insulating material: an old carpet, sacking or bundles of straw or bracken, for instance.

A rather different approach to the design of outdoor enclosures is to build lean-to glass cases against an upright, south-facing wall. This type of cage usually takes up less space than a full-scale outdoor vivarium, and so it may be possible to build a series of them in a fairly small area. This allows for the accommodation of a greater number of species, or of more than one breeding group of a single species. Although floor space is reduced, many species of lizard will use the back wall for basking, and climbing plants can be trained up this to enhance its appearance and to give the lizards some hiding places. At the front, the glass is most conveniently held in strong aluminium frames, and it should be possible to remove at least part of the front section without allowing the lizards to escape. Plate 3 illustrates a simple design which can be adapted according to requirements. Because it will be easier to catch the lizards in a small enclosure, it may be better to bring them indoors to heated accommodation during the winter rather than building a hibernaculum, although there should always be a place where they can shelter during unexpected cold weather.

PLANTING

Plants will be an attractive addition to the enclosure as well as providing shelter and hiding places for the lizards. Outdoor enclosures provide a great deal of scope for imaginative planting. Most set-ups

3.   A series of small outdoor vivaria, such as these built by Harry Baird in Holland, can be used to house a variety of small, hardy lizards. The fronts of the enclosures are south-facing.

will contain at least one area of rockery and this can be planted with a selection of alpine and rockery plants, all readily available. These should include plenty of the more robust species such as the cushion and mat-forming *Saxifraga*, *Sempervivum*, and *Armeria* (thrift), the hardier forms of *Sedum* and *Crassula* and a selection of shrubby species such as the dwarf willows, *Salix*. If a damp area is included, the larger, clump-forming *Primula* species offer a wide selection. Enclosures containing acid soils can be planted with heathers, of which there are a huge number of varieties, and one or two small *Azalea*, *Rhododendron* and *Pieris*, but all of these should be pruned back if there is any danger of the lizards climbing up them and leaping out of the enclosure.

All the above plants are suitable for cooler climates, i.e. areas where there is likely to be frost for a number of nights during the year. In warmer climates the plants listed for desert and semi-desert vivaria can be used (see Chapter 5), together with some of the species which would normally grow too large for indoor cages.

MANAGEMENT

Feeding the lizards in such an enclosure can present something of a problem because any insects which are introduced will quickly disperse, but the lizards will soon learn to approach a designated area of the enclosure if food is placed there regularly. The odd insect escapee will rarely cause any problems as the lizards will prevent feral populations from starting up. More of a problem can be the tendency of big lizards to eat little lizards. Large individuals will hunt young of their own species as well as smaller species, and communities should be built up with this in mind. Under normal practice, eggs which are found in the laying site should be removed regularly to be incubated elsewhere and the hatchlings are best housed indoors where their conditions and food supply can be better regulated. Only when they are of adult size should they be introduced into the enclosure. Even then, new males will often be harried to death as they attempt to find a territory in an already occupied area. The solution to this problem is to dispose of all surplus males, or to ensure that there are no surplus males by incubating the eggs at an appropriate temperature (see the sections on temperature dependent sex determination, in Chapters 1 and 7).

Other maintenance should be minimal; one of the advantages of keeping lizards outside is not needing to clean them out! Plants which have become straggly or which are on their way towards providing a means for the lizards to climb out, should be cut back and, if they are too vigorous, can be dug up and replaced with a slower-growing species. The pool may require occasional topping up during the warmer months, and a complete clean every autumn. With luck, the most time-consuming task will be the collection of eggs from the egg-laying site.

CHAPTER 5

Natural Vivaria

One of the most pleasing aspects of lizard-keeping is the possibility of creating natural or semi-natural cages for the animals. These range from cages with a layer of gravel on the bottom and one or two large rocks scattered about, to the most artistically arranged simulation of the species' natural habitat. They can include natural items such as rockwork, driftwood and, for the less boisterous species, the use of living plants within the cage. The skill necessary to create such cages combines the expertise of the reptile-keeper with varying amounts of artistic flair. In some cases a degree of horticultural skill and knowledge will also be an asset.

Although nothing can set off a group of lizards as well as a beautifully designed cage, the lizards' physical requirements must be considered above all other aspects. By choosing plants from a similar environment to that of the lizards the correct conditions for both can be provided without a conflict of interests. Indeed, some purists prefer to keep only those species of plants which are found with the lizards in the wild, and there is a case for this argument because these species will have exactly the same requirements regarding light, humidity and temperature. It does, however, tend to place an unnecessary constraint on the choices, both of plants and of lizards.

It goes without saying that all the considerations listed under heating, lighting and humidity in Chapter 3 should be read and borne in mind when designing a natural vivarium. Although vivariums can provide ideal conditions for plants, being in effect miniature hothouses with complete environmental control, specialised plants, which will be ones of most interest in this context, can be just as demanding to keep healthy as specialised lizards. There are plenty of books and magazine articles which can be consulted for information on general cultivation, and it is often helpful if the plants are kept for house decoration for a while so that their requirements and suitability can be assessed.

The most simple way of growing plants in a vivarium is to place a layer of pebbles, gravel or Hortag over the base of the cage and stand potted plants directly on this. The effect is not exactly natural, but maintenance is straightforward, mistakes can be easily rectified by changing the plants, and the lizards will benefit from the additional perches and hiding places. In order for a more natural set-up to work on a long-term basis, much more planning is necessary, and it may be best that the lizards are not housed in the cage until the plants have settled in and are growing happily – often many weeks or even months after they have been planted. Each plant should be thoughtfully positioned, taking into account the amount of light and water required as well as the aesthetic aspects of the 'landscape'. It is probably true to say that an ambitiously planted cage will not work for long unless there is some interest in the plants in their own right.

Apart from general disturbance, the other problems which can lead to the downfall of the plants include being eaten by the lizards or by insects such as crickets which have been introduced as food, lack of drainage, scorching by heaters and lack of light. Some of these pitfalls can be avoided by compromising slightly. If the plants are kept in their pots, and these are plunged into the substrate, many of the problems can be avoided. In this way, plants which fail to thrive can be removed without disturbing others and possibly replaced with more tolerant species. Similarly, if the plants do *too* well they may need to be removed and replaced with less vigorous species. Despite the potential problems, an intelligent approach to planting the cage will go a long way towards making the set-up look attractive for many months if not permanently – the plants may outlive the lizards!

The final choice of plants, types of rockwork and substrate will depend largely upon the environment which is being created, but before going on to discuss particular types of set-up, a few practicalities should be discussed. Much the same rules apply to plants' requirements as to lizards', and advice given in the previous chapters will apply to both. However, plants have other requirements, not covered there. In particular, most plants require drainage, and this can be a problem in a sealed cage. The most effective way around the problem is to start building the set-up by first placing a layer of coarse gravel, crocks or Hortag on the bottom of the cage. (Hortag is a horticultural product consisting of small clay beads used for crocking pots or greenhouse staging.) Pots containing plants will then be placed directly on to this layer and be raised above the level of any standing water. The cage substrate, which may consist of gravel, leaf mould, moss peat, etc. is then packed around the pots so that their rims are hidden. The same substrate can be used for topping off the pots so that the plants appear to be growing directly from it. Any rockwork, dead branches and so on should be partially buried in the substrate rather than placed on the surface, where they will look unnatural.

Lighting should be tailored to the plants as well as to the lizards. While lizards benefit from ultra-violet radiation, plants do not. They require light from the warmer end of the spectrum, especially red light. Therefore, the ultra-violet fluorescent tube, if used, must be supplemented by one producing a warm light. Special growth tubes are available from horticulturalists, but any tube having a yellowish or pinkish emission will usually be adequate provided its intensity is sufficient. Plants which are getting insufficient light will be elongated, pale in colour and will bend towards any nearby window or other strong light source. Trial and error is often the only way of arriving at the right quality and quantity of light.

Temperatures suitable for the lizards will probably be equally suitable for the plants assuming that appropriate species have been chosen. Underfloor heating is ideal for plants, and is used exclusively these days in plant propagation. Spotlights, light-bulbs and other powerful radiant heat sources will quickly dry out and scorch any plants in the vicinity. If these types of heaters are used in the set-up the plants will need to be positioned at the opposite end of the cage. Humidity will usually take care of itself inasmuch as lizards and plants

4.   A selection of small succulents suitable for desert or semi-desert vivariums.

from similar environments will have similar requirements. Note, however, that although many tropical plants benefit from regular spraying and a high humidity, desert plants such as cacti will quickly rot if water is allowed to lodge in their centres or around their bases.

Although many plants have very specific requirements and are relatively difficult to keep alive for very long, there are also several species which may be thought of as 'survivors'; plants which will continue to grow in the face of the most appalling adversity. Fortunately, there seem to be a few of these to suit each type of environment, and so, provided the lizards are small and are not herbivorous, and the plants are not placed directly under a powerful heater, it should be possible to grow at least something in almost every cage.

DRY DESERT ENVIRONMENTS

A good number of lizards come from desert habitats and these often make very suitable captives. Species which bask during the day, such as the side-blotched lizards, *Uta*, collared lizards, *Crotaphytus*, and the zebra-tailed lizard, *Callisaurus*, require powerful spotlights or ceramic heaters as well as plenty of ultra-violet, and it may be necessary to

5.   An unidentified species of *Stenodactylus* from Egypt, possibly *S.petrei*. Small desert species such as this are especially suitable for housing in a natural desert type of terrarium.

restrict plants to a shady corner of the cage, perhaps wedged amongst a jumble of rocks. Nocturnal desert lizards, mostly geckos such as the eublepharids *Eublepharis*, *Coleonyx* and *Hemitheconyx*, or the typical geckos *Teratoscincus* and *Geckonia*, do not require such intense heat and thrive in a natural set-up. Substrate in all such cages will usually be gravel or sand, or lava (natural or artificial) may be used. If rocks are also used, try to find pieces which are similar in colour and texture to the rest of the substrate as this will give a more natural appearance.

Many of the commonly available succulent plants will look at home in this type of cage. They should all be watered with care and both their pots and the substrate in which they are plunged should drain freely. Several of the choice species of *Crassula*, such as *C. ausensis* and *C. socialis* are available from specialist succulent nurseries and sometimes from garden centres. *Crassula argentea* is the well-known jade plant, with a gnarled trunk and round, fleshy, green leaves, and *C. lycopodioides* forms a clump of slender stems covered with scale-like leaves: these latter two species are the 'survivors' which will often grow where all else fails, as will any of the *Bryophyllum* species, which reproduce themselves prolifically by forming tiny plantlets along the edges of their leaves.

Other suitable species include many of the more succulent *Aloe*, *Haworthia* and *Gasteria* species from South Africa and the *Dudleya*, *Echeveria* and *Agave* species from North America, although members of the latter genus may eventually grow too large for the average vivarium. Several of the fascinating mimicry plants, such as *Lithops* and *Pleiospilos*, thrive under hot dry conditions but their requirements are rather specialised. Related South African genera, such as *Mestoklema*, *Faucaria* and *Drosanthemum* are more accommodating. Cacti, which all come from North or South America, are obvious choices for certain types of set-up, especially those housing American desert lizards, and are easily available from garden centres, but the smaller clump-forming species, with soft spines, such as certain *Mammillaria* and *Astrophytum* species, are less of a menace than the larger species of prickly-pears or barrel cacti. The genus *Euphorbia* contains a bewildering variety of different species, some of them very similar to cacti in appearance (through convergent evolution). Several of the more succulent species, such as *E. balsamifera* and *E. milii* are tough and well-suited to vivarium planting. Species forming a swollen caudex, such as *Ibervillea sonorense* from North America and *Fockea edulis* from South Africa are interesting curiosities and, although not always freely available, are tougher than many other species because they store considerable water and nourishment which can tide them

Fig. 4.   Desert vivarium, containing two small *Aloe* species.

over periods of stress – indeed, most plants of this type should be given a dry resting period for about six months of the year so that they stay firm and compact.

SEMI-DESERT VIVARIA

Many lizards come from areas which have what geographers call a 'Mediterranean' climate. These include such species as the southern European wall lizards, *Podarcis*, and also species from other parts of the world where similar conditions prevail, such as many of the spiny lizards, *Sceloporus*, the swifts, *Leiolaemus*, and the whiptails, *Cnemidophorus*. Nocturnal species such as many of the geckos, especially the *Hemidactylus* species, and several crepuscular skinks such as the western North American species of *Eumeces* and the European and North African *Chalcides* species are also found in this type of habitat. Vivaria set up for these and similar species will be rather like those for desert species but should include one area which is kept slightly moist. For the skinks, especially, there should be an area of leaf-litter or a pile of bark fragments in which they can hide and hunt. This area should be sprayed occasionally to raise the humidity.

Several of the plants listed above will also thrive in this environment, provided they can tolerate the rather more humid conditions brought about by occasional spraying. In addition, less succulent species such as young *Nolina*, *Yucca* and *Dracaena* species will survive, as will the succulent figs such as *Ficus petiolaris* and *F. palmeri* for those fortunate enough to be able to obtain them. Smaller plants suitable for these

37

Fig. 5.   Forest vivarium, planted with species such as *Philodendron* and other 'house plants'.

conditions include the bulbous *Scilla violacea* which is sometimes used as a house plant, and very many *Sedum, Echeveria* and *Crassula* species.

TROPICAL FOREST VIVARIA

Surprisingly few diurnal basking species come from tropical forests, and those that do, such as the common iguana and the water dragons, *Physignathus*, are far too large and active for a planted cage to remain intact for very long (and many of them eat plants anyway). The selection of lizards, then, is limited mainly to smaller species such as the geckos, especially the day geckos, *Phelsuma* and *Gonatodes*, and to the smaller iguanids such as the many *Anolis* species.

This type of vivarium fits most people's idea of what a tropical rainforest should look like! However, the cage should not be dripping wet all the time – this will not suit the lizards or any of the plants suggested here. Regular spraying is necessary, but ventilation should be good so that the humidity is allowed to fall between sprayings. A very effective method of maintaining the correct degree of humidity is to have running water in the cage. A small circulation pump can be used to force water to the top of a miniature waterfall and the spray from this will create perfect conditions for many plants, while those requiring rather less humidity can be planted further away. Similarly, the lizards can move about according to their demands.

Many of the plants which are sold as houseplants will thrive in this type of environment, although some may prove to be too rampant under the ideal growing conditions of a heated vivarium. Many of the best choices are found among the epiphytes. These are plants which grow on other plants, and may be conveniently attached to pieces of driftwood or rock rather than planted in a pot. The most familiar epiphytes are found among the bromeliads, or air-plants, and the orchids. Air-plants tend to be less expensive and often look rather more robust than orchids. They may be attached to cork bark, dead

6.   A beautifully planted rainforest terrarium, complete with running water, at Rhenen, Holland. This particular set-up would probably be rather too humid for many lizards, but would suit small geckos such as the South American *Gonatodes* species.

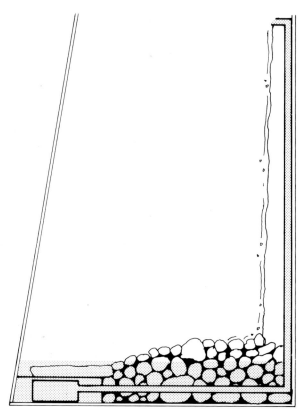

Fig. 6. Running water raises the humidity of a cage and can be arranged by installing a small circulatory pump and arranging the rocks to form a small cascade.

wood or rocks with aquarium sealant, or they can be tied-in using sphagnum moss and nylon thread. They require good ventilation and only an occasional light spraying – many species are found in fairly dry situations and they sometimes rot if they are kept permanently damp. Position them near a ventilation panel to prevent water from lodging between their leaves. They die after flowering but usually send out offsets, until eventually a small clump is formed. Spanish 'moss', *Tillandsia ursnoides*, is a small bromeliad which hangs from branches and which can be used to good effect – again, it should not be kept dripping wet.

Of the orchid species, those belonging to the genera *Odontoglossum*, *Pleurothallis* and *Brassia* are just a few examples of small-growing species which are not too demanding. The very showy hybrids which are often sold in plant centres and florists are useless for vivarium planting. A small species of flamingo plant, *Anthurium*, is sometimes available and this will grow well if attached to a piece of cork bark or driftwood and sprayed regularly. There are a few species of epiphytic ferns which lend themselves especially well to vivaria and these include the well-known bird's-nest fern, *Asplenium nidus*, while the club mosses, usually sold under the generic name *Selaginella* will form a good ground cover. If all else fails in this type of vivarium, good standbys include the smallest umbrella plant species, *Cyperus diffusus*, and the peace lily, *Spathiphyllum*. For very tall cages, the larger umbrella plant, *Cyperus alternifolius*, is spectacular, but it may grow to a height of five feet or more. The umbrella plants will thrive if their pots are stood permanently in an inch or two of water, and they are useful for semi-aquatic cages used to house the few species of lizards such as the Chinese crocodile lizard, *Shinisaurus crocodilurus*, which require this kind of habitat. For rather drier situations any of the ivies, *Hedera*, species of *Peperomia* or *Maranta*, the spider plant, *Chlorophytum comosum*, the dumb cane, *Dieffenbachia* or species of *Tradescantia* are almost indestructible.

Although insectivorous plants such as the venus fly trap, the sundews and the pitcher plants will thrive in the warm and humid environment of a vivarium, they will compete with lizards for food and large specimens may even 'eat' small lizards! They are therefore best kept on the windowsill.

CHAPTER 6

Food and Feeding: the Menu

As a group, lizards have a wide range of food preferences. There are totally herbivorous species, totally carnivorous species and species which will eat both plant and animal material. Carnivorous species range from generalist insectivores, eating more or less anything which moves and is small enough, to highly specialised species such as those which only eat molluscs or ants. Several of the larger carnivorous species will accept carrion, i.e. dead animals, and may be trained to eat minced meat or dog- and cat-food from a dish. As a rule, variety in food is the key to the successful keeping and breeding of lizards, but it is unrealistic to expect to be able to supply as great a variety as the lizard would have access to in the wild, and so vitamin and mineral supplements are often required in order to maintain a balanced diet. In addition, those species which obtain their vitamin D3 via sunlight require a satisfactory substitute (see also the section on lighting in Chapter 3).

HERBIVOROUS SPECIES

Several of the larger iguanids and agamids are at least partially herbivorous. *Iguana iguana*, for instance, will, when adult, thrive on a diet consisting exclusively of plant material, provided that this is of the right type and is suitably supplemented. Other species, such as the bearded dragons, *Pogona*, will also accept a fairly high proportion of plant material in their diet when adult, but also require insects.

Any fruit or vegetables offered to lizards should be washed to ensure that it is free from insecticides, etc. and the same applies to leaves which have been collected for feeding. Since some individuals seem to have firm preferences it is sometimes helpful to chop the food up and mix it together, otherwise they will refuse all but the favoured items and may suffer from lack of variety. On the other hand, they may still

7. Many of the larger herbivorous species, such as these iguanids, will eat chopped fruit and vegetables from a bowl. Vitamins and minerals can be simply sprinkled over the meal.

sort through the mixture, rejecting unwanted material and there is very little that can be done about this. Vitamin and mineral powders can easily be sprinkled on to this type of food and mixed in well, especially if the food is still wet from washing. The actual amounts and the precise formulation of the supplement will vary according to species and to whether or not they are provided with an ultra-violet basking source, but several of the proprietary brands are designed for reptiles and, in the absence of specific information, which is rarely available, the dose rates supplied with the goods should be a good starting-point. Any changes in the health or the behaviour of the lizards may require an adjustment of the feeding regime.

LARGE CARNIVOROUS SPECIES

Species such as monitors, tegus, the large Australasian skinks and heloderms consume large quantities of food, and offering live insects to species such as these would be impractical and expensive. Prey items can include dead mice, rats and chicks, or the animals may be trained to accept canned pet food. The latter often makes a good diet because, apart from the convenience of storing and feeding it to the animals, extra vitamins and minerals are often part of the formulation and, even if they are not, these can be added easily. Many large lizards will eat eggs and, although this often makes for messy cages, it is a good, readily obtainable standby which, again, can be easily fortified with other substances. Young individuals of these species can be treated as small insectivorous lizards, and even adults seem to benefit from occasional feedings of large insects, such as locusts.

SMALL INSECTIVOROUS SPECIES

The majority of lizards which are offered for sale fall into this category. Included are all the geckos, wall lizards, most skinks, chameleons, anoles and many others. These species require a constant supply of suitably sized insects if they are to remain healthy and breed. Although a small number of insect species are easily cultured, and some of these are commercially available, it appears that few, if any, of them can be regarded as a complete diet for any species and so lizards should all be fed with a variety of cultured insects, as many wild insects as is practicable and vitamin and mineral supplements. The notes regarding lighting in Chapters 1 and 3 should also be studied.

As a rule, small lizards should be fed every day, although it will not matter too much if they miss the odd day. Only enough insects should be put in the cage for the lizards to eat all or most of them before they are fed the next day and if there are still insects left over the next day, food should be withheld. Tipping large numbers of insects into a cage and hoping that they will keep the lizards supplied with food for a long time is not good practice. If living plants are used in the cage this is doubly important because many of the insects used as food will destroy or mutilate plants if left in the cage for any length of time.

INSECTS AS FOOD

The following species of insects are the ones of most use to lizard-keepers. Some notes on their culture are given so that small breeding nuclei can be maintained for use in emergency, but if large-scale production is planned then more detailed culture methods should be sought elsewhere. Most of the food items listed are readily available through reptile dealers, pet stores or by mail order.

Mealworms *(Tenebrio molitor)*

Mealworms are the larval form of a flour beetle and are amongst the easiest of food-insects to culture. Their value as food is suspect, however, because they are low in digestible calcium, and lizards that are fed on them exclusively soon develop defects.

Setting up a breeding colony consists of placing 100–200 mealworms into a large plastic box or tray with a layer of chicken-meal on the bottom. Vegetable peelings, in small quantities, can be added to provide moisture. The mealworms will eventually pupate and then emerge as adult beetles. Eggs will be laid in the medium or in crumpled newspaper or sacking if this is laid over the culture. At a temperature of 25–30°C these will hatch and develop into large mealworms in about three months. In order to keep a constant supply it may be necessary to set up a number of cultures, harvesting them in rotation and using a proportion of the mealworms to start a new generation.

Waxworms *(Galleria mellonella)*

Waxworms are the larval form of a moth which is a serious pest of beehives. They are favoured by practically every species of lizard and appear to be a valuable food when used as part of a mixed diet. They will, unfortunately, climb straight out of a cage which is not covered, pupate around the house and emerge as a plague of moths after a few weeks. For this reason they are best fed directly to the lizards, most of which will soon learn to chase and catch them as they are thrown into the cage.

Breeding waxmoths is not too difficult. They require a medium of wholemeal flour with added yeast (in a ratio of approximately 20 : 1) moistened with a mixture of equal parts honey and glycerine. This should be added gradually until the medium is crumbly. A small piece of purchased waxworm culture (or a piece from an older culture) is placed in a hard plastic lunch-box on top of a one-inch layer of the medium. Ventilation to the container should consist of panels of *very fine* metal gauze in the lid. When the moths emerge they will mate almost immediately and the females will lay strips of eggs in the crack between the lid and the box. These can be removed with a fingernail and placed on top of some fresh medium in another box. The larvae are very tiny when they first hatch (hence the need for very fine gauze) but grow rapidly if kept warm (25–30°C). As they burrow through the medium they spin webs which bind it together into a single clump, and this can be broken open to collect larvae for feeding. Additional medium should be added as the larvae consume their way through the food supply. A small clump of medium, containing about twenty or so larvae should be used to start the next culture, and any surplus can be stored for a few weeks if they are kept cool (10–15°C).

Tebos

Tebos are moth larvae which are not cultured but which are harvested in tropical countries and exported as animal food. They are similar in appearance to waxworms and are equally relished by the lizards. They are sometimes available through the more specialised reptile (and tropical bird) suppliers.

Crickets

Two species of crickets are commonly cultured as food for insectivorous lizards. The best known of these is the house cricket, *Acheta domesticus*, a small, light brown species which may become established in the house under warm conditions, and the field cricket, *Gryllus bimaculatus*, which is approximately twice as large as the house cricket and dark brown, almost black. The latter species is not so prolific, but is a more useful food for larger lizards and will not live for very long if it escapes indoors. Both these species are cultured in the same way and there are doubtless other species which would be equally useful.

To most people, crickets are most conveniently purchased as required. This saves valuable time and space and avoids much of the risk of escapees becoming a nuisance. Because they are now so readily available, through pet stores or by mail order, there is a danger that they will be used almost exclusively, and this should be avoided. A vitamin and mineral supplement should, as a rule, be sprinkled over the crickets before they are fed to the lizards and only a small number introduced at one time so that the lizards can mop them up before they have a chance to clean off the powder. This will also avoid the possibility of their setting up home somewhere out of reach of the lizards and feasting off the plants which have been used to decorate the cage or, even worse, any eggs which the lizards have laid.

Any suitably sized container may be used to culture crickets provided it is escape-proof – they are unable to climb perfectly smooth surfaces so a lid is not strictly necessary provided the sides are kept clean. A layer of sawdust may be placed on the floor of the container although this is not essential, and plenty of crumpled newspaper, cardboard boxes and so on should be scattered over the floor to act as territories. Adult males stridulate (sing) by rubbing their forewings together, whereas females are silent. The latter may be recognised by a long ovipositor protruding from the end of their abdomen. They will eat most cereals, but powdered chick meal or chick crumbs are probably the most economical way of feeding them. Vegetable scraps or grass can be added to this. The females lay their eggs in any damp substrate and this can be provided in the form of a shallow dish containing vermiculite, peat or cotton-wool. After one or two days the dish is removed and replaced with another. The dishes containing eggs should be covered to prevent them from drying out, and placed somewhere warm. When the young crickets hatch they can be released into a fresh container and fed until they are a suitable size for use. The complete life-cycle takes about three months at 25°C, and if a number of breeding cages are set up in rotation crickets of varying sizes will be available at all times.

Fruit flies

The laboratory fruit fly, *Drosophila melanogaster*, has limited use as a lizard food because of its small size. However, it may be necessary to use them from time to time for feeding newly hatched lizards. It should be possible to buy starter cultures complete with the medium and a population of fly larvae. If these are kept warm a number of flies will hatch each day and these can be fed directly to the lizards. Once the culture is exhausted it is better to buy a fresh one rather than attempt to breed further generations as this is time-consuming and messy.

Other live foods

A variety of other species of live food, usually insects, is often available commercially. These include locusts, maggots, buffalo worms and other species. All are useful as part of a balanced diet, but none makes a satisfactory diet if fed exclusively. Some, such as locusts and giant mealworms, are especially useful for the larger lizards. Sometimes, reptile-keeping goes hand-in-hand with an interest in entomology and this can be a useful combination as surplus insects, such as stick insects, can form a welcome additional food supply.

Several of the medium to large lizard species are not averse to accepting small vertebrate prey such as young mice. Few would consider it worthwhile to breed rodents for the sole purpose of providing lizard-food, but if these items are available, and the lizards can be persuaded to accept them, they make an excellent food.

COLLECTING FOOD

Many lizard-keepers overlook the plentiful (and free) source of food which may be collected near to their homes or in their gardens. Although there is some danger of contamination by insecticides, pesticides and other -cides, insects found away from roads and agricultural land are usually clear of these chemicals, and if they are numerous this is a good sign that they have not been sprayed. The best method, wherever possible, is to rely on the invertebrate population which quickly builds up in a patch of garden which has been untended. This could be part of a 'wildlife gardening' project, with native wildflowers, or it may just be a neglected patch of nettles and other weeds whose existence can thus be justified!

Insects are most easily collected by using a sweep net or butterfly net, which is passed through the undergrowth a few times, and then flipped over to trap the insects in the bottom of the net. Another successful method, especially for catching spiders, is to fill a string bag with straw, dead leaves or crumpled paper. This is placed amongst the undergrowth for a few days, then placed inside a large polythene bag and shaken vigorously. It will be found that large amounts of lizard food will drop out into the bottom of the bag, and the 'trap' can be replaced ready for another harvest. If necessary, the catch, from either method, can be transferred to jars, and possibly sorted, before being fed to the lizards. In order to avoid large insects being introduced to the cages the centre of the lid can be cut out and a disc of wire mesh fixed into place. The gauge of the mesh should be such that only suitably sized insects will pass through when the jar is shaken. Any large insects left in the jar should be returned to the weedy patch from whence they came – big insects produce little insects!

VITAMIN AND MINERAL SUPPLEMENTS

Hardly any lizards can be maintained in captivity without supplementing their food with certain vitamins and minerals. This is necessary because wild lizards have access to a wide variety of foods which, together, provide the correct elements in suitable proportions. In addition, sunlight is important, for some species at least, in the production of some vitamins.

Unfortunately, our understanding of lizards' dietary requirements is very poor and, although formulae have been established for the successful feeding of certain species, there is no general rule which can be applied to all species. Bearing this in mind, the best strategy seems to be to provide a broad spectrum of supplements in the hope that each lizard will obtain from it that which is lacking in its diet; the mix will not be exactly right, but it won't be exactly wrong either. To this end, various manufacturers have produced supplements which can be used fairly confidently. These vary from purely vitamin additives to substances containing only minerals, but most contain some of each and are intended as complete dietary supplements. In addition, several successful lizard-breeders have developed their own formulae for the species they are most interested in and some of these contain a proprietary product as well as other more basic substances.

Only supplements formulated specifically for reptiles should be used. Products intended for other domestic animals such as humans, dogs and cats are unlikely to contain the correct proportions of vitamins and minerals. It may be necessary to use two or more supplements in order to provide everything the lizard requires. Most mixtures contain adequate trace elements, and so the most important ingredients to look out for are calcium, phosphorus and a range of vitamins. As a rule, powdered supplements are more stable than liquid ones, and it is easier to ensure that the animals are consuming at least a reasonable amount, which is not always the case when liquids are added to the water bowl, for instance.

Powders may be added to the food of insects for about one week prior to their being fed to the lizards and this will boost their food value dramatically. Alternatively, one day's ration of insects can be placed in a small polythene bag with a teaspoon of the powder and shaken up until they are liberally covered. If the insects are first chilled they will be less active and so less likely to clean the powder off before they are eaten, as well as being easier for the lizards to catch. If the same bag is used every time, any remaining powder will not be wasted. For herbivorous lizards, the powder can simply be sprinkled over the food after it has been prepared.

Calcium and phosphorus are important constituents of bones, and calcium also plays an essential role in the nervous system. Furthermore, dietary calcium and phosphorus must be present in the

49

correct ratio, which ranges from approximately 2 : 1 for herbivorous species and up to 20 : 1 for carnivorous species. Many insect foods are poor in calcium, or contain calcium which cannot be absorbed by lizards. Most vegetable material is also low in calcium but high in phosphorus. Phosphorus is therefore much more readily available through normal diets than is calcium and the correct balance must be restored. For this reason, a supplement which is high in calcium is usually essential. A few proprietary mineral supplements contain extra large amounts of calcium for this reason and these can be used with a fair degree of confidence. Alternatively, a general purpose mineral supplement can be fortified by adding an equal quantity of extra calcium in the form of calcium gluconate or calcium lactate. A more natural alternative is to provide a separate source of calcium in the form of ground cuttlefish bone or crushed egg-shell and many lizards will actively seek out and eat these in order to balance their calcium requirements. Small dishes of these substances are simply placed in the cages and replenished when empty. This is a particularly good method of providing extra calcium to females which are forming eggs, especially geckos, which lay hard-shelled, calcarious eggs. Other suitable supplements include those which contain calcium and vitamin D3 together (see below). Symptoms of calcium deficiency include loss of motor reflexes, with total paralysis in extreme cases, and deformed skeletons (kinked backs or tails, knobbly spines and bent limbs).

Vitamin D3 is essential for the assimilation of calcium. No matter how much calcium is present in the diet, without vitamin D3 the lizard cannot use it to form bone, and so symptoms of vitamin D3 deficiency are identical to those of calcium deficiency. There are two ways to overcome the problem. A natural spectrum fluorescent light source can be used to provide the ultra-violet necessary for vitamin D3 synthesis (as described in the section on lighting in Chapter 3), or vitamin D3 can be given as a dietary supplement. Note that if the latter course is chosen, vitamin D3 is not the same as the vitamin D which is included in human vitamin pills or drops – this is vitamin D4, and is not suitable for reptiles. The recommended dose rate for vitamin D3 is 50–100 International Units (IU) per kg per day. Unfortunately, this is almost impossible to calculate in practice since the amount consumed by the lizards will depend on how much falls off the food before it is eaten. Suffice to say that a supplement high in vitamin D3 should be liberally dusted on to insects or vegetables fed to lizards every feed or every other feed. The addition of a blacklight or other ultra-violet source will enable the lizard to make up for any slight deficiency in its diet. Please note that it is possible to overdose calcium and vitamin D3: an excess of these substances will lead to the formation of bony material where it is not wanted – outgrowths along the backbone and calcification of the arteries, for instance.

Other vitamins which are often deficient in captive diets include vitamins A, C, E and several of the vitamin B complex. Under normal circumstances, animals will obtain small quantities of all these from a varied diet, and show little or no ill effects from any slight deficiencies which may arise, but under periods of stress, especially when breeding, these may lead to reduced resistance to disease, swollen eyes and poor hatch-rate in eggs. Supplements which are high in these vitamins can be used as a standby, but are not normally necessary as a matter of course.

CHAPTER 7

Breeding

Breeding is the most satisfying aspect of lizard-keeping and should be the aim of everyone who keeps them in captivity. An animal which is kept in isolation is biologically dead, and the practice of buying a single animal as a 'pet' should be condemned as adding to the problems which are brought about by wholesale and indiscriminate collection of wild animals for the pet trade. The establishment of breeding colonies of the most popular species could eventually satisfy the greater part of the demand for lizards, and silence critics who regard reptile-keeping as a serious threat to the survival of certain species in the wild.

Many species are already protected and trade in several others is restricted. Far from putting limitations on the activities of amateur enthusiasts, this highlights the problems which populations of wild animals are facing and should encourage a more serious approach to the hobby, with more research into the correct conditions for keeping lizards well.

Great progress has been made in the search for successful regimes for the breeding of certain species of lizards, but not so great as in other branches of herpetoculture, especially snake-keeping. Part of the reason for this is probably connected with the vitamin D3/calcium problem outlined in the previous chapter, allied to the fact that the various groups of lizard species each require a rather different approach. We do not yet have a 'formula' for breeding lizards and, owing to their variation, never will have. General advice on breeding can only cover basic principles and techniques.

SEXING

Telling the sex of a lizard ranges from very simple to almost impossible. At its most straightforward, the secondary sexual characteristics, shown by many species, are so obvious as to be recognisable at a great distance. These consist of the crests, horns, dewlaps and brighter coloration present in males. The function of these ornamentations is associated with their visually orientated social systems and serves to signal ownership of a territory to other males and to attract females. In almost every case, juveniles are coloured like females, and only sexually mature animals can be distinguished by these characteristics. As males mature they often become larger and more powerful than the females, especially around the neck and jaws. This characteristic is due to sexual selection: in territorial animals, which often need to fight for the right to feed and mate, natural selection acts upon the males in such a way that genes for aggression and a powerful physique are perpetuated. In non-territorial species these characteristics are not apparent, while in females and juveniles, the need for camouflage is often the strongest selection pressure.

In many families of lizards, males can be recognised by the presence of a series of pores, either on the inside of the thighs (femoral pores) or immediately in front of the vent (pre-anal pores), or both. Once again, these become more obvious as the animal matures but slight differences can sometimes be detected even in juveniles.

Males of some species, most notably the geckos, have a very obvious swelling at the base of the tail. This is caused by the presence of the paired hemipenes, which are inverted into a sac which opens on to the cloaca. When mating takes place one or other of these hemipenes is

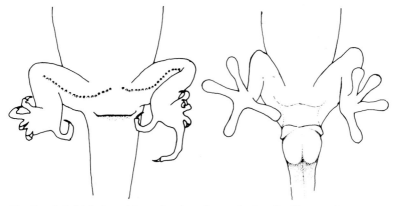

Fig. 7. *Left*: Male lacertids, and males of several other families, can be distinguished by the presence of a row of pores along each thigh and immediately in front of the cloaca: females either lack these altogether or they may be less obvious.

Fig. 8. *Right*: Distinguishing the sexes in geckos is usually straightforward: the males have a prominent bi-lobed swelling at the base of the tail.

53

everted (pushed out) by blood pressure. The swellings of the hemipenal sacs can be seen when the ventral surface of the lizard is examined. With geckos, this is often best accomplished by encouraging the animal(s) on to the glass front or sides of the vivarium, avoiding the need to handle them. Other species may show slight differences in the shape of this region of the tail, although rarely so clearly as in the geckos. Occasionally, it may be possible to evert the hemipenes manually by applying pressure to the base of the tail with a thumb. This is, however, a rather difficult technique and rarely works with adult animals. Similarly, probing the hemipenes with a smooth blunt instrument (such as the probes specifically designed for probing snakes) is of limited use in the case of lizards.

By observing these secondary sexual characteristics, it is possible to sex many species of lizards by the time they are mature. With other species, however, in which the sexes are not so distinct, it may be necessary to obtain a small group of animals and rear them together, in the hope that behavioural differences will arise as they mature. At this point it should become obvious which are the males. Alternatively, if the animals are of a less territorial species it may be possible to keep a small group together more or less permanently and allow them to breed as a colony.

Finally, it should not be forgotten that many species of lizards show temperature dependent sex determination: it may become possible to decide in advance the sex of the offspring simply by selecting the appropriate incubation temperature (see Chapter 1). This predictability is equally useful whether the offspring are for increasing your own stock or for disposal to other lizard-keepers.

MATING SYSTEMS

In nature, most species of lizards probably live in more or less discrete colonies, where one male controls a territory containing suitable habitat and a good food supply. This territory is shared by one or more females and, sometimes, a number of juveniles of either sex. If adequate space is available, captive breeding systems can replicate this arrangement, and set-ups of this type are natural for the lizards and interesting for the lizard-keeper. Unfortunately, the required space is rarely available, except perhaps in outdoor enclosures, and a compromise has to be sought. The majority of lizards are best housed in single pairs or in breeding groups consisting of one male and two or three females. In small cages, the male may assert himself rather too vigorously and it may become necessary from time to time to remove females in order to restore their general condition and reduce stress – spare cages should be available in case this is necessary.

Under these circumstances, the lizards will normally mate at a time which corresponds with their breeding season in the wild, normally spring, but some species, notably those from the tropics, may breed continuously throughout the year. Either way, it will be necessary closely to monitor the females for signs of developing eggs or young and either to remove them before these are produced or to make provision in the cage.

CONDITIONING

Before breeding can take place successfully the animals must be in peak condition. Most lizards have evolved a social system based on a single territory-holding male and one or more female consorts. This situation (along with other factors such as temperature and daylength) promotes the urge to reproduce, and breeding behaviour may be suppressed if the animals are not allowed to behave naturally in this respect. It is therefore of prime importance to take note of their territorial needs and to provide the space and conditions in which these needs are satisfied.

Males which are in good breeding condition can often be recognised by brilliant colours and bold behaviour; they will often commandeer the most prominent 'landmark' in the cage and display constantly to

8. Lizard eggs can be incubated in a small container of moist vermiculite.

other individuals of the same and other species. Conditioning of the females entails regular feeding with a good quality diet and, in particular, plenty of calcium. This is necessary for the formation of the shells, in the case of egg-laying species, or of the skeleton of the embryo, in live-bearing species. Lack of calcium will lead to poor shell formation, resulting in lack of viability of the eggs, inability of the young to break out of the shell (dead in shell) or deformed hatchlings. Live-bearing species will give birth to dead and partially developed young or the young will be undersized, weak and short-lived. There is good evidence that calcium deficiencies are accumulated over several generations: in a long-term breeding programme the young will become progressively weaker and the incidence of deformities will increase. Once the fault is corrected, the hatch rate and vigour of the young will improve dramatically. It is important therefore to understand the part played by vitamin D3 in the assimilation of calcium and to understand the importance of the calcium:phosphorus ratio. (See Chapters 1 and 6.)

EGG-LAYING AND BIRTH

Females that lay eggs will seek out a damp place in which to bury these, and this can be catered for by placing a box of damp peat or peat/sand mixture in a secluded corner of the cage. It should be inspected regularly in order to check for eggs and to ensure that the material has not dried out. Once eggs are found they should be removed from the cage to be incubated separately.

Live-bearing species will usually find a quiet spot in which to give birth. Although there is a danger that other adults in the cage will attack and eat the young this should not occur if they are well established and adequately fed. An alternative method is to remove the pregnant females and leave them in a separate cage until the young are born, but this may subject them to stress. The relative advantages and disadvantages of the two methods should be weighed up in each individual case, taking into consideration the temperament of the species concerned and past experiences with the same or similar species.

INCUBATION OF EGGS

Eggs which have been removed from a breeding cage must be incubated at a steady temperature and provided with a suitable substrate. Most lizard eggs are soft-shelled and must absorb water throughout their incubation. They should be placed in a plastic box with a layer of moist vermiculite. The correct mixture is approximately one part water to three parts vermiculite but the exact proportions may vary according to the grade of vermiculite used. In general, it should be moist throughout, without being waterlogged. If the eggs are separate they should each be placed in a small depression in the vermiculite (most conveniently made with a finger) but if they adhere together in a cluster no attempt should be made to separate them as damage may result. The box in which the eggs are to be incubated should be covered with a lid, but a few small holes should be made so that a small amount of air can enter. There should be no need to add further quantities of water during incubation but the box should be checked from time to time. Eggs which are infertile tend to be of an unhealthy yellow colour, whereas fertile ones are pure white or pinkish. Infertile eggs will soon become attacked by mould and can be removed, assuming they are not in the middle of a clump of good eggs, in which case it is probably better to leave them where they are (healthy developing eggs are rarely attacked by mould although the surface of their shells may discolour). Just before hatching the eggs may start to collapse, or they may 'sweat'. This is normal in some species and they should not be discarded unless all hope of healthy hatchlings has been abandoned.

Gecko eggs (except those of eublepharid geckos) are not soft-shelled like those of other lizards and do not need to absorb moisture throughout incubation. This is probably an adaptation which allows them to lay their eggs away from the ground, hidden behind loose bark or amongst stones. Captives often stick their eggs to a plant, rock or the side of the vivarium and it may be impractical to remove them for incubation. In this case it will be necessary to protect them by taping a small plastic container over them, and removing the young when they have hatched. If the eggs are loose they can be removed and placed in an incubator. It is not necessary to use vermiculite although it is advisable to place the eggs on a thin layer of sand or pebbles in order to prevent them from rolling around. The eggs of some species appear to hatch better if they are lightly sprayed from time to time and it may be that the young require a certain amount of humidity in order to break out properly.

As has been noted in Chapter 1, the temperature at which the eggs are laid may determine the sex of the young (temperature dependent sex determination). It is not known how widespread this phenomenon is amongst lizards but it has been demonstrated in most geckos and also in species in several other families. When there is any doubt, it

9.   Gecko eggs are heavily calcified: this young tokay, *Gekko gecko*, has just hatched.

may be advisable to divide the clutch of eggs and use several different temperatures if this can be arranged. By keeping accurate records it will eventually be possible to correlate temperature with sex and, if there *is* an effect, the derived values can be used in the future to manipulate the sex ratio.

REARING HATCHLINGS

It is rarely possible to rear young lizards in the same cages as the adults. They should be housed in a separate vivarium with similar conditions to those of the adults but more simply arranged (so that their progress can be monitored more closely). Hatchlings of small species require large quantities of small insects and it may be necessary to culture these in order to be assured of a constant supply. Vitamins and minerals are especially important, as is ultra-violet light in those species which would normally bask. The young of most species will live as a group, at least until they approach sexual maturity, but sometimes, for instance with day geckos, *Phelsuma* species, there will be conflict between individuals and they will each require a separate cage. Although time-consuming, this is the only way in which a reasonable survival rate can be expected.

As a rule, captive-raised lizards adapt much better to captivity than wild-caught individuals and become relatively tame. Furthermore, they are more likely to breed successfully.

INBREEDING

Where lizards are bred on a fairly large scale, for instance the leopard geckos and the bearded dragons, the dangers of inbreeding begin to increase. Inbreeding depression is the term used to describe the effect of lethal genes accumulating in a population and affecting the survival and vigour of the animals. It can be avoided by crossing out to unrelated animals every two or three generations. Where it is not possible to obtain new blood (if the species is protected, for instance) efforts should be made to contact other keepers breeding the same species with a view to exchanging some stock. If the colony has been started with a large enough group of animals it may be possible to avoid inbreeding depression for many generations by using a maximum avoidance breeding system. This entails keeping records of each young produced and creating a pedigree chart. In future generations, the least related young should be paired.

CHAPTER 8

Health and Management: Staying in Shape

Keeping a stock of lizards healthy has more to do with common sense and a basic understanding of their biology than with an intimate knowledge of veterinary science; veterinary surgeons and successful lizard-keepers alike agree that prevention is much better than cure, especially where cures may be hard to find. The first pitfall which beginners must learn to avoid is the choice of unsuitable species; it is an unfortunate fact that the prettiest lizards are often the most difficult to keep. Species such as the chameleons, the agamas, anoles and horned lizards, to name but a few, are terribly difficult to keep healthy for any length of time and most experienced lizard-keepers steer well clear of them. Beginners, on the other hand, are often tempted by their bright colours or interesting shapes and their first adventure into lizard-keeping is doomed before it begins.

Like all animals, lizards suffer from a number of diseases, some of which may be fatal. In captivity, however, they are unlikely to 'catch' a disease; after all, the viruses and bacteria causing disease in lizards have to come from somewhere and there are not too many sources of these in the average home. Almost all problems associated with the health of lizards is related to incorrect husbandry. Maintaining healthy stock, therefore, consists of four basic rules:

- choose carefully the species you intend to keep
- ensure that the animals are not infected when they are obtained
- research their requirements and ensure that these are met
- keep them free from infection by quarantining any new additions before they are introduced to established stock

Before approaching a dealer or breeder, you should know which species it is that you are interested in, where it comes from and what its requirements are. Take into account its ultimate size; there is absolutely no point in purchasing a young monitor or iguana, for instance, unless it can be adequately housed when it is adult. There is little or no second-hand market in reptiles that have outgrown their accommodation. Many lizards are difficult or impossible to keep unless you are prepared to make a large investment in specialised equipment and time. Often, the cost of the cage, heating and lighting equipment will exceed, by far, the initial cost of the lizard. If this is likely to be a problem, choose another species which is less demanding – it is far more rewarding to maintain a small group of unspectacular but healthy individuals than one large sick specimen of a species whose requirements you are not able or prepared to meet properly. Look upon your purchase as a long-term commitment, with the ultimate aim of producing some captive-bred offspring.

Specifically, beginners should consider species such as the leopard gecko, *Eublepharis macularius*, any of the house geckos, the smaller species of skinks or captive-bred bearded dragons for their first purchase. All of these species have been shown to be fairly easily kept in captivity under relatively straightforward conditions.

Lizards offered for sale are either bred in captivity or caught from the wild. Captive-bred stock is the least likely to carry infection and should be preferred over wild-caught stock whenever possible. Captive-bred animals always adapt to captivity better than wild ones and, perhaps more importantly, the fact that someone has bred a species indicates that its requirements are unlikely to be too demanding. Unfortunately, only a small number of lizard species are bred in reasonable numbers and the choice will therefore be limited. Joining one of the many herpetological societies aimed at amateur reptile-keepers is the best way of locating people who are active in the field of captive-breeding.

Lizards collected from the wild are more usually obtained through specialist reptile dealers or from retail pet outlets. Often these animals have been kept under unsuitable conditions from the moment they are collected until they are offered for sale – sometimes several months. They may carry infections but, more often, any diseases they are suffering from will be the result of stress. Wherever possible, stock should be inspected prior to purchase; buying lizards by mail order, unless they come from a totally reliable dealer, is always a gamble.

Having chosen a suitable species, and before choosing individual specimens, it is helpful to get some idea of the general standard of husbandry carried out by the dealer. Are the cages clean and properly labelled? Do they contain bowls of clean drinking water? Are there pieces of shed skin and faeces lying around? Has any attempt been made to isolate and give treatment to animals which are obviously thin? These factors are far more important than the extent of the stock, the number of rarities offered for sale or the prices.

Having established that the general upkeep of the establishment is acceptable, turn your attention to the species you have chosen to purchase. Look first for any signs of external injury: damaged snouts, missing toes, torn skin. The nostrils should be clear and the eyes bright. Check for swellings or cysts on the surface of the body and limbs and for blisters or patches of discoloured scales, especially on the ventral surface, which may be due to fungal infection caused by damp conditions. Specimens of certain species, especially geckos, will often have regrown tails as a result of fighting or predation in the wild, but recently broken tails may be caused by poor handling.

Wild lizards should not be 'tame'. Specimens that can be handled without a struggle are not usually tame, but lethargic. This can simply be the result of having been kept too cool, or it may be caused by disease and should be looked upon with suspicion. If possible, try to be around when the lizards are fed; the healthy individuals will be those that go straight to the food and eat. Now look for the sexes; often, the most brightly coloured specimens will be males – don't take more than one of these unless they are of a species which is known to be non-territorial (hardly any). The fact that they seem to be living together in harmony in a cage in a pet shop is no indication of how they will behave when they are established in a more permanent cage. Quite often they are stressed through overcrowding and their natural intra-specific aggression is suppressed. It will surface again just as soon as conditions improve. Finally, don't assume that the accommodation in the pet shop is suitable for the species in question; often these cages are only intended for short-term housing and are aimed more towards displaying the animals attractively than keeping them healthy and happy.

All the above precautions must be carried out before any lizards have actually been obtained. One further arrangement must be made: the cage should be built, set up and running before the animals are brought home. In certain circumstances it may be possible to house the lizards temporarily in an aquarium or other easily obtained container while their permanent home is put together. If the lizards are to be added to an existing group, or if other species are already established, new arrivals will need to be put in quarantine unless you are *very* sure that they are free from infections. This involves keeping them in a separate cage or, better still, a separate room from other lizards, and housing them in a simple cage with minimal furnishings: often a substrate of paper towels, a small water bowl and a cardboard box for them to hide in are the basic requirements, together with some means of maintaining the correct temperature range. This quarantine cage should be serviced after all other lizards, and any items of equipment used, such as water bowls, feeding forceps, etc. should be sterilised before they are used in other cages. Once the new lizards are eating regularly, and assuming their faeces etc. are normal, then placing them in their permanent home can be considered, but bear in mind that recently infected animals may harbour parasites and diseases for several months before showing any clinical or behavioural signs. Adding new stock to an established collection is *always* risky; these risks can only be minimised if great care is taken to select clean, healthy stock. Never, ever, buy obviously diseased animals from a pet dealer, even if they are cheap (or free).

Now that a healthy stock of lizards has been obtained, the correct environment must be created if they are to stay healthy. Precise details of these requirements for various species and the ways in which these can be met are described elsewhere in this book, but, to summarise, captive reptiles must have access to:

- a suitable temperature or, better still, a range of temperatures (see Chapters 1 and 3)
- a suitable diet, usually including extra vitamins and minerals (see Chapter 6)
- fresh drinking water, either in a bowl or sprayed on to their cage, plants within the cage or their own skin
- a suitable light source and, usually, a source of ultra-violet light (see Chapters 1 and 3)
- a diurnal and seasonal light rhythm (photoperiod) which equates with that normally found in their place of origin (see Chapter 3)
- possibly living plants, rocks or other furnishings to provide hiding places and basking sites (see Chapters 3 and 5)
- the opportunity to establish territories and live without continual harassment from dominant individuals (see Chapter 1)

If all these requirements are met adequately there should be no reason why the lizards should not live out their normal lifespan, and many will breed. Day-to-day routine husbandry will vary greatly with species. In general, small lizards require feeding every day or every other day. Where appropriate, they should be sprayed with water every day, sometimes twice a day, especially if they are species which are reluctant to drink from a bowl, e.g. Chameleons and *Anolis* lizards.

Large species may also require daily feeding, especially if they are herbivorous, but some need only weekly feeds. Natural set-ups require very little in the way of daily maintenance, other than to keep the glass front of their cage clean and to ensure that water bowls do not become fouled. It may be necessary to cut back plants occasionally and plants which have grown too large for the cage, or have died, will need replacement with something more suitable. Large lizards kept under simple conditions may need regular cleaning – daily in the case of certain carnivorous species such as monitors – if their cages are not to become dirty and smelly. All these tasks must be carried out as common sense dictates and there are no hard and fast rules to be followed. For most people, part of the pleasure in keeping lizards, indeed any caged animals, is to ensure that they are attractively set up and maintained. If the tasks develop into a chore it is likely that the collection has become too large or the initial novelty of keeping lizards has worn off; in either case, disposing of or reducing the collection should be considered.

Complete sterilisation of cages, water bowls and so on should not be necessary except under dire circumstances, such as the aftermath of a disease epidemic. Regular or occasional disinfection is sometimes practical on a limited scale and can be helpful. Glass cages can be thoroughly washed and wiped out with a weak solution of domestic chlorine bleach or one of the proprietary disinfectants marketed for reptiles. Water bowls can be stood in a similar solution and it can be a good idea to have two water bowls for every cage so that they can be used in rotation and disinfected in the meantime. Note that practically all disinfectants are neutralised in the presence of organic matter, so cages, bowls and other equipment should be thoroughly washed *before* they are disinfected. Even elaborate set-ups must be broken down and all soil, logs, stones and plants disposed of if a serious infection has been present. Although such drastic action is rarely necessary it is a very good reason for ensuring that all animals introduced to such a set-up are free from diseases or parasites.

Lizards which become 'sick' will normally need treatment by a veterinary surgeon. Very few vets are familiar with reptiles or the diseases which afflict them and so it may be necessary to travel some distance to find one that is. Again, membership of a society may be useful in finding the right vet. Many vets, though not experts on reptilian diseases, will take an interest and go to great lengths to establish a satisfactory course of treatment. Fortunately, lizards are fairly tough animals and will usually survive for a while until a cure is found. It is a mistake, however, to wait until they are at death's door before advice is sought, because recovery will then, at best, be lengthy and possibly incomplete. If the disease has been caused by incorrect feeding or husbandry, or by intra-specific fighting, it is obviously important to correct these conditions immediately; although a vet may be able to cure the clinical results of poor husbandry, correcting the underlying causes are the responsibility of the owner.

DIY treatment involving the use of antibiotics is not to be recommended. The hobbyist's part in disease control consists of maintaining the correct environment, in which case disease will rarely occur, and of recognising abnormal behaviour and the other symptoms of disease as soon as possible. Look especially for animals which suddenly cease feeding or which do not bask. Males may lose their bright colours when the breeding season ends but this can also be due to health problems. Pieces of skin which remain attached after shedding has taken place should be removed by hand but if the problem occurs repeatedly it is likely that the conditions are too dry or the animal is not in good condition. Blocked nostrils or a mucus discharge from the mouth and nostrils are symptoms of respiratory disease, which may in turn be caused by an incorrect temperature. Loose faeces, most noticeable in large lizards, are often caused by a diet which is lacking in fibre. This often arises in herbivorous species, the digestive systems of which are often adapted to the most tough and seemingly indigestible plants possible: try feeding the skins and throwing away the fruit!

Bone deformities are not so easily corrected unless they are spotted immediately. The symptoms, consisting of weak and deformed jaws, crooked spines and tails and paralysis of the hind legs, are the result of a combination of deficiencies. Many species require ultra-violet light in order to convert the pre-vitamin D3 (from their diet) into vitamin D3. Without this they cannot assimilate calcium and other essential elements into their skeletons and nervous systems. Lack of calcium, or an incorrect calcium : phosphorus ratio, will obviously have the same result. Almost all lizards must have a plentiful source of vitamin D3 and/or ultra-violet light *and* calcium and this is particularly important for breeding females. Detailed information on this most important subject will be found in Chapters 3 and 6.

External parasites can sometimes be seen on the skin of wild-caught lizards. Although the damage they cause is usually minimal they can be instrumental in transmitting disease from one animal to another. Mites are very small and can sometimes be seen moving, as small shiny specks, over the surface of the lizard especially around the eyes, but they are more often spotted as a result of their grey, dust-like

10.   Small lively lizards should be grasped firmly but gently behind the head while the body is supported in the hand.

droppings. They can be eliminated by placing a small strip of Vapona in the cage. It should be kept out of reach of the lizards (and their food) by enclosing it in a small perforated plastic tub, and removed after three or four days. Two weeks later the treatment should be repeated in order to kill any mites which have hatched in the meantime, and a third exposure may be necessary before the infestation is finally eliminated. Ticks are much larger and flattened in shape. They attach themselves to the skin of the lizard by means of specialised mouthparts and cannot be removed simply by pulling them off. Vapona will kill ticks as well as mites but ticks can more easily be removed by first dabbing them with a paintbrush dipped in methylated spirits, then carefully gripping them with tweezers and flipping them over while tugging gently.

Internal parasites consisting of worms and flukes are often

11. Moving delicate species from cage to cage is sometimes best achieved by allowing them to crawl on to the hand; this is less likely to cause stress.

harboured by wild lizards. Again, these do not often cause serious problems unless their populations become unbearably large. This is most likely to occur when the lizards are under stress. The worms, or their eggs, will be detected in the lizard's faeces by a veterinary laboratory, and an appropriate anti-helminth given. Some vets insist on administrating this themselves but others will provide the substance and give instructions on its use. Assuming the lizard is feeding it is less stressful to use the food as a vehicle for the drug rather than to give it via a stomach tube or an injection. Other internal parasites include the protozoan *Entamoeba invadens*: infestations of this will lead to loss of weight, often accompanied by regurgitation, loose faeces covered in

67

mucus, and convulsions. Infected animals rarely recover unless they are treated immediately and the disease is highly infectious. Note that enteritis caused by *Salmonella* infections can also give similar symptoms and these are fairly easily treated (and often clear up spontaneously if the lizard is kept warm and disturbed as little as possible).

In concluding this rather daunting chapter, it is worth reiterating that *almost all ailments suffered by captive lizards are due to an incorrect environment and poor husbandry.*

CHAPTER 9

The Eublepharid 'Geckos'

The eublepharids, long considered to be primitive geckos, are now placed in a family of their own, the Eublepharidae, although they are still popularly known as geckos. Although this is a small family, consisting of only 18 species, they have a worldwide distribution, suggesting a formerly much more successful existence. They are now found in North and Central America (the *Coleonyx* species), Central Asia (*Eublepharis* species), West Africa (*Hemitheconyx* and *Holodactylus* species), Japan (*Goniurosaurus* species) and Malaysia (*Aleuroscalabotes felinus*).

Eublepharids differ from true geckos in having eyelids. None of them have expanded pads on their digits and, with the exception of the little-studied *Aleuroscalabotes* and *Goniurosaurus* species they are ground-dwellers, typically living in desert and desert-fringe areas. All are nocturnal.

Members of three genera are frequently kept and bred in captivity. These are *Eublepharis*, *Coleonyx* and *Hemitheconyx*. The other species are only rarely seen and then only in the collections of specialist 'gecko-philes'.

Housing for all these geckos is simply arranged. They do not require a large amount of space and a 60 × 30 × 30 cm vivarium is satisfactory for a small group of adults. As they do not climb there is no need to fit a lid to their cage unless crickets are to be used as food. Substrate can consist of almost any dry material, but most collectors prefer a semi-natural arrangement of sand or fine grit, with a few stones for interest. The geckos should have a place to hide, either a cave formed with flat rocks or an artificial hidebox consisting of an upturned plastic box with an entrance cut in one side. Water must be present at all times. A daytime temperature of 25–30°C should be aimed for, with a slight drop in temperature at night. This is not critical – in the wild these species often withstand extremely cold night-time and winter temperatures. Heating is most conveniently arranged by using an underfloor heat mat or heat tape, or the room in which they are kept can be heated. Overhead heating by way of a light-bulb or spotlight also works, although the geckos will rarely bask and the bright light may prevent them from being active during the day. The sand in one part of the cage should be lightly sprayed occasionally so that the geckos will have ample opportunity to move into an area of high humidity should they require it – if an upturned clay or plastic box, with an entrance hole in one side, is placed over this patch of damp sand the moisture will be retained longer and the dark, damp microclimate so created with facilitate shedding. Failure to do this will often result in pieces of skin remaining around the toes, and infection may set in if the problem is not corrected.

Food can consist entirely of insects (crickets, waxworms, mealworms, sweepings, etc.) or this can be supplemented with newborn mice for the larger species. Some individuals will relish the latter while others will steadfastly refuse to have anything to do with them. A supplement containing vitamin D3 and calcium should be given occasionally: about once each week for young animals or for females which are breeding, slightly less for adult males. Alternatively, a small dish of grated cuttlefish bone can be placed in the cage and the animals can then take as much as they need. Many (perhaps all) of these geckos need to ingest considerable quantities of sand and, unless this is used as a substrate, a small bowl of it should be placed in the cage and replenished when necessary.

Males tend to grow larger than females and can also be distinguished by their larger, more powerful heads and necks and the presence of hemipenal sacs at the base of the tail. In males of the *Coleonyx* species there are curved spurs projecting outwards from the base of the tail. Hatchlings and juveniles can be difficult to sex, although there is some slight difference in the arrangement of the pre-anal pores, the young males having a V-shaped row of small pores in front of the cloaca. Adult males cannot be kept together because they are extremely aggressive and will fight until only one remains. Females are not territorial and so the best method of housing a breeding group is to keep one male together with a number of females, one to four being a good ratio for a medium-sized cage, although higher ratios, e.g. one to eight, can be used if required.

Breeding takes place from early spring onwards and continues well into the summer. Each female will lay four or five clutches of eggs each season, with an interval of about one month between each clutch. It is rarely necessary to do anything to induce breeding – if the animals are

12.   The leopard gecko, *Eublepharis macularius*, is the perfect lizard for keeping and breeding in captivity and is highly recommended for beginners.

housed in breeding groups all the time they will start to breed as soon as the daylength increases. Alternatively, the males may be kept in small separate cages and each female introduced in turn. Mating then often takes place immediately, after which the female can be removed and placed in another cage for egg-laying – this procedure is more time-consuming and less natural but may be useful for certain projects in which precise breeding data is required. Females which are about to lay are easily recognised by their swollen abdomens and, if they are carefully turned over, two large white patches can be seen through the abdominal wall.

The eggs are laid in pairs and, unlike those of the true geckos, have soft shells. The females will seek out a patch of sand which is moist

71

and this should be provided, for instance in a shallow plastic box, around the time of egg-laying. Again, it can be useful to place an upturned bowl or tray over this container to prevent the sand from drying out too quickly and to give the females some seclusion. The eggs are buried by the female and the laying area must be inspected daily if the eggs are to be harvested for incubation (especially necessary where more than one female is kept in the same cage, as subsequent females often dig up or otherwise disturb eggs laid previously). The collected eggs can be incubated in damp sand or vermiculite and the temperature at which they are kept will determine the sex of the offspring. In the species which have been studied so far, an incubation temperature of 27–29°C produces females and one of 32–33°C produces males. The eggs hatch in 6–12 weeks, depending on the temperature selected, and the young geckos live off their yolk sacs for the first few days, after which they will shed their skins. There is rarely any point in offering food before this occurs. After they have shed they are usually lively and keen to eat small insects. With good care and feeding they can become mature within one year, although two years is more realistic. Youngsters often fight if they are overcrowded, leading to the loss of tails and weak, stressed individuals. This can be avoided if they are kept in small groups with adequate hiding places.

Representative species

It is most appropriate that the species accounts begin with the leopard gecko, *Eublepharis macularius*, the species which effectively turned lizard-keeping into lizard-breeding. In 1979 the *International Zoo Yearbook* published a paper (Thorogood and Whimster, 1979) describing a remarkably successful system for housing and breeding leopard geckos under laboratory conditions. Until this date, practically all lizard-breeding had occurred more by accident than design and no long-term breeding projects had been considered feasible. Partly as a result of this paper, the leopard gecko is now bred in truly huge numbers and captive-bred juveniles are freely available at reasonable prices through the pet trade.

It is a medium-sized species growing to a total length of about 15 cm, of which slightly less than half is tail. The surface of its skin is roughened by numerous small warty growths (tubercles) and the basic colour of adults is yellow to tan, with patches of chocolate brown spots. Juveniles are more strikingly marked, being yellow with four or five solid bands of chocolate brown and a black and white banded tail. The bands gradually break up as the animal grows, until the more spotted adult coloration remains.

Three of the species of *Eublepharis* are found in Central Asia, including one truly gigantic species, *E. angramainyu*, which grows to a total length of over 30 cm, but these are never offered for sale. If this situation changes, and any of them become available, there is no reason to suppose that their care and breeding will differ to any great extent from that described above.

Three other species of eublepharid geckos are known from Asia. Two of these, now placed in the genus *Goniurosaurus* , but formerly regarded as members of the genus *Eublepharis*, occur on the Japanese islands of the Ryukyu archipelago (*G. kuroiwae*) and on islands in the Gulf of Tonkin, China (*G. lichtenfelderi*). Neither species are well-known, either in the wild or in captivity but *G. kuroiwae* at least is known to be a cave dwelling species. This species also occurs in several distinct colour forms, sometimes regarded as subspecies. They require a fairly high humidity but otherwise their care in captivity appears to follow that described for the other eublepharid species.

The third Asian species, *Aleuroscalabotes felinus*, is known as the cat gecko and is found on the Malaysian peninsula and in Borneo. It apparently lives an arboreal lifestyle in tropical rainforests, making it unique amongst the eublepharids, but almost nothing is known about its care in captivity except that there appears to be great difficulty in keeping it alive.

The African fat-tailed gecko, *Hemitheconyx caudicinctus*, is a large, heavily built gecko from the desert regions of northeastern Africa. Its coloration consists of a few broad, alternating chocolate brown and tan bands on the body, a less distinctly banded tail and, in a proportion of specimens, a narrow white or cream line running from the top of the head to the base of the tail, cutting across the transverse bands. Inheritance of this striped characteristic seems to be genetically determined. In captivity it requires identical conditions to the leopard gecko, both with regard to general maintenance and to breeding, but this species is not always as easy to handle and may bite – hard! Although the original imported individuals were rather difficult to adapt to captivity, captive-bred juveniles have proven almost as easy to rear and breed from as those of the leopard gecko, making this an excellent alternative to that species.

Another species of *Hemitheconyx*, *H. taylori*, is known from East Africa, and two other eublepharids, belonging to the genus *Holodactylus*, have also been described from the same region. As far as is known, these species have never been imported and are certainly not generally available.

13. Juvenile leopard geckos are more boldly marked than adults.

Seven species of *Coleonyx* are recognised, ranging from North American desert regions down into the forests of Central America. They are known as banded geckos and are the New World counterpart of the leopard gecko, although generally smaller. Several species live amongst rock piles in and around the deserts of southern North America and hunt small insects at night, whereas the Central American species occur in more humid forest regions. Their care in captivity is similar to that described above, but all the banded geckos are rather more delicate and should be handled with care. A small glass or plastic cage should be used, with a 5 cm layer of sand or fine grit as a substrate. A pile of rocks at one end will provide places for the geckos to hide and will give an attractive, semi-natural appearance. Temperatures should be 25–30°C with a slight fall at night.

Banded geckos will usually feed readily on crickets, although only

14. Banded gecko, *Coleonyx variegatus*.

15. The banded gecko, *Coleonyx variegatus*, is an attractive and easily cared for species from the deserts of southwest North America.

small numbers should be placed in the cage at a time. Waxworms, moths and small spiders probably form a better diet. A multivitamin supplement containing vitamin D3 and calcium should be dusted on to the food occasionally. Water, and a damp area, should be present at all times.

Sexing these species could not be easier. Male banded geckos have short thorn-like spines projecting at right angles from the base of their tail. They also have a hemipenal swelling in the same region. Females which are carrying eggs are also most obvious, the thin translucent skin of the back and, especially, the underside, allowing the developing eggs to be clearly seen, often without the need to handle the lizards. The eggs are laid in damp sand and should be treated as described above, but although sex determination of the young is almost certainly temperature dependent no figures are available and so a range of

76

16. The barefoot gecko, *Coleonyx switaki*, is an attractive but rare relative of the banded gecko.

temperatures should be used in order to prevent the production of only one sex or the other. The temperatures given for the leopard gecko would be a good starting-point, with adjustments made for subsequent clutches if the desired effect has not been achieved the first time. The boldly banded hatchlings are very small and have a frail appearance, but rearing them should not present any real problems provided that

77

an ample supply of suitably sized soft-bodied insects or spiders are available.

Several subspecies of the western banded gecko, *Coleonyx variegatus*, are recognised. All grow to about 10 cm of which about 40 per cent is tail. The skin has a soft velvety texture, without tubercles, and is pale cream in colour with well-defined bands of mid-brown. The eyes are large and are protected by prominent eyelids.

C. brevis and *C. reticulatus* occur in southern Texas and adjacent parts of Mexico. The former is rather smaller than the western banded gecko, its bands are not so distinct, and adults are peppered with small brown spots. *C. reticulatus* is large, growing to about 15 cm in total length, and has rough skin, more like the leopard gecko. It is a rare species, only having been discovered in 1956. Neither of these species is freely available but their care in captivity is similar to that outlined for *C. variegatus.*

Also rarely seen, but most spectacular in appearance, is the barefoot gecko, *Coleonyx switaki* (formerly known as *Anarbylus switaki*). This species is found in the extreme southwest corner of California and in Baja California. It, too, lives in piles of rocks and is rarely collected. Its skin is roughly tuberculate and the markings consist of dark grey or brown ground colour with round spots of white, cream or yellow, these spots sometimes arranged into rows runnuing across the body. The tail is boldly banded in white. Few captive specimens exist but it appears to adapt well to captivity, requiring similar conditions to other North American eublepharids.

The two strictly Central American species, *Coleonyx elegans* and *C. mitratus* are rarely seen in captivity. They are both attractively marked, with chocolate brown and tan markings on a creamy background, and have tuberculate skins. Again, their care in captivity follows the usual pattern for eublepharid geckos but these species must be given an area of damp sand which must not be allowed to dry out. This is best arranged by making an artificial cave, either of rocks or an upturned plastic box with a hole cut in one side, and regularly spraying the area over which it is placed.

CHAPTER 10

Geckos

The true geckos form a large family of over 800 species distributed throughout the warmer parts of the world. They are characterised by fused eyelids (the eye being covered with a large, transparent scale) and granular scales. Many species have expanded adhesive digits allowing them to climb smooth, vertical surfaces. Their eggs are rounded, hard-shelled (calcareous) and always laid in pairs in the larger species, singly in the smaller ones.

Many geckos make amusing and rewarding subjects for the vivarium, and many will breed in captivity under fairly basic conditions. Because of the great diversity of species, with their differing origins and requirements, I have divided them into five groups in order to simplify the notes on their care and breeding: typical geckos, small desert geckos, day geckos, sphaerodactyline geckos and diplodactyline geckos.

1: TYPICAL GECKOS

Typical geckos may be thought of as those that conform to the general family description above and are fairly generalised in their habits and lifestyle. Nearly all are nocturnal and many have become associated with Man, often inhabiting houses, restaurants, hotels and other buildings, especially in the tropics, and are commonly known under the collective term 'house geckos'.

Although not all species discussed here have expanded toe-pads, most can climb well and cages for them must be well covered. Many habitually live a vertical life, hunting for insects on tree trunks and rock-faces or on the artificial 'rock-faces' which humans conveniently provide in the form of walls and ceilings. These latter species also capitalise on the abundant food supply provided by insect pests in houses, such as flies and cockroaches, and often learn to forage around lights in the evening, when large numbers of flying insects are attracted. Most of these nocturnal species communicate by vocalisations, the word 'gecko' being an alliteration of the call of house geckos.

Many of these species are worthy of consideration for the vivarium. Although not all of them are colourful, they are interesting and entertaining. More importantly, they usually adapt very well to a captive environment, live for a long time and will often breed readily. They need tall cages with plenty of vertical surfaces such as those provided by branches and upright slabs of rock. Failing these, they will cling to the sides of the vivarium. The type of substrate on the cage floor is not too important in many cases, but an attempt should be made to match this to the natural habitat of the species, i.e. gravel for the rock-dwelling species, bark chippings or leaf-litter for the forest species. Living plants can often be used to enhance the cage and, again, these should be of appropriate species – succulents for species from drier habitats, leafy species for those from forests.

The cages should have a background temperature of around 20–30°C for most species and lighting should be subdued. Most species will become active during the early evening provided that the cage is not too brightly lit, and this is the best time to feed them as they will then mop up the insects as soon as they are introduced. Crickets are a good staple diet, but other items such as waxworms and sweepings should be given as often as possible. Every meal should be fortified with a vitamin/mineral powder, dusted on to the insects immediately before they are introduced to the cage. Unless the geckos are willing to eat as soon as the food is introduced into the cage it is a good idea to place the food in a smooth-sided bowl after first clipping the crickets' hind legs – this prevents them from escaping to nooks and crannies and cleaning off the vitamin/mineral powder before they are eventually eaten. Many geckos prefer to lap drops of water from leaves, rocks or the sides of the cage, and so a thorough spraying every day is advisable. Ventilation should be good, however, so that the cage dries out within a few hours of spraying.

Many of the tropical geckos will breed throughout the year provided they are in good condition. Others begin to breed in the spring and continue laying eggs right through the summer. Breeding pairs or groups should be kept together permanently, although males, and sometimes females, are usually territorial and will need to be kept separately. Eggs are always laid in pairs, except in the case of a few very small species which only lay a single egg. The eggs are calcareous and gravid females will require large quantities of calcium at breeding time.

This is best provided in the form of a high calcium/vitamin D3 supplement dusted on to the food, but small pieces of cuttlefish bone left in a bowl or petri-dish in the cage will also be taken in most cases. Females will store this extra calcium in the paired calcium sacs in their throat region, where it can be seen as a raised white mass showing through the translucent skin. Most species attach their eggs to wood, rock or the vivarium sides. Sometimes they are hidden, for instance beneath a piece of loose bark, but very often they are laid in an exposed position. Attempting to remove the eggs usually results in damage and the best policy is to remove the object to which they are attached, if this is practicable, and place the whole lot in another cage for incubation. Alternatively, and especially if the eggs are attached to the sides of the vivarium, a small plastic cup or box can be taped over them so that they are protected from predation by the adults in the cage and so that the newly hatched young can be caught and moved to a rearing cage before they disperse throughout the breeding cage, often to disappear forever. Other species bury their eggs in sand or gravel and these are easily removed to a separate incubator until they hatch.

Note that in all the species studied so far the sex of young geckos is determined by the temperature at which the eggs are incubated. Precise data is not available for all species but a good starting-point would be to incubate some eggs just above 30°C and others just below this temperature, which seems to be critical for at least some species. Depending on the results obtained from this method, the temperatures could be modified until the desired sex ratio is obtained. Unfortunately, it is not always possible to sex young geckos and it may be necessary to wait until they approach sexual maturity before the results are known.

Young geckos of similar sizes can often be reared together, but if there are signs that fighting is taking place, or if one or more animals are getting the lion's share of the food, then they must be reared separately. The ideal containers for young geckos are small plastic lunch-boxes. These should have the minimum of cage furnishings, just a suitable substrate and a small piece of bark under which they can hide. Food, in the form of small crickets, etc. should be introduced often, and in small quantities, and should be liberally dusted with vitamin/mineral powder. Sexual maturity can be attained within a few months for some of the small species but may take as long as two years for the larger ones.

17. *Gecko vittatus*, a strikingly marked gecko from New Guinea, closely related to the more common tokay (Plate 9).

Representative species

Owing to their almost ubiquitous occurrence, geckos of this type are imported frequently from most parts of the world. As such a huge variety exists, and as many of them are difficult to identify accurately (especially if their origin is not known), only the more distinctive species can be described here, but the care of most species will be similar. The most important factors which contribute towards the welfare of geckos in captivity are humidity, temperature, vitamin and mineral supplementation and secure daytime hiding places, especially vertical cracks and crevices. If the animals are not thriving it is likely that one or more of these conditions is not suitable and it may be necessary to experiment until the animals are happier.

One of the largest geckos, and one which is frequently offered for sale is the tokay, *Gekko gecko*. This robust species seems to have fallen from popularity recently, probably because it is difficult to handle without receiving a painful bite! It makes an interesting subject, however, not least because it is tough and undemanding in captivity and breeds readily. Tokays, which grow to 30 cm or more in length, are slate blue in colour with an even sprinkling of orange spots. The males vocalise raucously, and the name 'Tokay' is a fair imitation of their call. Tokays require a large vivarium with lots of vertical surfaces

18. The flying gecko, *Ptychozoon kuhli*, is an Asian species which breeds readily in captivity.

19. Moorish gecko, *Tarentola mauretanica*, from the Mediterranean region.

created, for instance, by resting pieces of cork bark against the back and walls of the cage. They require a temperature of about 25–30°C although this is not critical, and a diet of large insects and small rodents. Any other small lizard kept in their cage will be eaten. Once a compatible pair or harem is formed the females will lay pairs of eggs regularly over several months. These are normally attached to a vertical surface, usually somewhere near the top of the vivarium. Incubation period varies enormously, with extremes of 100 and 200 days having been recorded: much of this variation is probably due to differing temperatures. Other species in this genus, such as *G. vittatus* and *G. stentor*, are occasionally seen and would appear to require similar conditions, although some of them are rainforest species which probably appreciate a more humid environment.

Other Asian species which are often available include the so-called flying geckos, genus *Ptychozoon*. At least three species are known and their appearance, lifestyle and care in captivity is similar. Their natural habitat is to live on vertical tree trunks, especially palms and other rainforest trees. If disturbed, they will launch themselves into the air, and folds of skin along their flanks and between their digits will open to slow their descent. The most common species, *P. kuhli*, grows to about 20 cm in length and males are distinguished by paired swellings at the base of the tail. They require a tall cage with thick boughs lodged vertically from top to bottom and a temperature of about 25°C. They readily accept the usual insect fare, supplemented as above, and quickly adapt to captivity. Only one male should be kept in each cage, preferably with a single mate. The eggs are laid every six weeks or so under good conditions and take about 100 days to hatch. The young will mature in less than one year if fed adequately.

The genus *Hemidactylus* is huge and wide-ranging, and some members have increased their distribution by stowing away in cargoes of timber, fruit and other materials. The Turkish gecko, *H. turcicus* occurs in southern Europe and parts of western Asia and is typical of most species. The skin is translucent and pinkish, with small tubercles covering the head, back and tail. These are white in colour and may be superimposed upon a number of irregular dark blotches. In captivity they prefer a fairly dry environment. They are most at home when provided with rocks and stones to climb upon. One or two robust potted plants will enhance the appearance of the cage and give the geckos plenty of places to perch and, if the soil in the pot is kept moist, they will be able to take advantage of the humidity gradient produced. Their cage should be lightly sprayed occasionally, when they will drink drops of water from leaves and rocks, although they will normally learn to drink from a small water bowl. They eat almost any insects which are small enough, such as crickets, waxworms and sweepings, and breed throughout the summer, attaching their two hard-shelled eggs to a rock or to the sides of their cage. Other common species in the genus include *H. brooksi*, Brooks' gecko or the Asian house gecko, which has a wide range and is also an efficient stowaway. This species is slightly smaller than the preceding one, but its care in captivity is similar. Like other members of the genus, it will breed prolifically, each female laying several pairs of eggs during short bursts of reproductive activity. The eggs hatch in about 50 days if incubated at a temperature of 32°C. Other species of *Hemidactylus* which may occur in the pet trade from time to time are often unidentified (or wrongly identified) but will usually thrive under the simple arrangement described above.

Another species with similar requirements is the Moorish gecko, *Tarentola mauretanica*, a Mediterranean species which is somewhat larger than most *Hemidactylus* species. It grows to about 20 cm in length and is greyish in colour. This species is likely to be found basking during the day, although its main period of activity is during the evening.

20. Kotschy's gecko, *Cyrtodactylus kotschyi*, a tough and attractive European species. Although bent-toed geckos do not have expanded toe-discs they climb well and should be given a pile of rocks or logs to clamber over.

Members of the genus *Lygodactylus* are amongst the smallest species and are usually known as dwarf geckos. They are found in southern Africa, Madagascar and South America and the species can be difficult to identify unless accurate locality data is available. They all appear to be undemanding, however, the greatest difficulty being the constant supply of small insects required, since the adults grow to only about 6 cm, and the hatchlings measure about 2 cm. These geckos are largely diurnal and appreciate a vivarium with plenty of perches to climb and bask upon. They are best kept as a small colony, with one male and several females, when the various social interactions can be observed. Young crickets and waxworms are the most convenient food and it may be necessary to culture these in order to obtain the small sizes required. Extra calcium should be available to the females. They will breed at almost any time of the year, the females laying their eggs in pairs over a six-month period if adequately fed. The eggs hatch in about eight weeks at a temperature of 28°C.

Members of the genus *Cyrtodactylus* are sometimes known as bent-toed geckos. They have no expanded toe-pads at the end of their digits but climb by means of hooked claws. Many species are found in Asia and one, *C. kotschyi*, occurs in Europe. This species has similar requirements to the other Mediterranean species, i.e. warm and dry, with a jumble of rocks to climb amongst, but several of the Southeast Asian species live in rainforests and require rather more humidity. Two species which are commonly imported are *C. pinguensis* and *C. pulchellus*. Both these species are brightly coloured, the former being tan with dark brown blotches on its back and a black and white banded tail, and the latter being banded in light and dark grey. They will only thrive in captivity if their temperature and humidity preferences are fully understood; they both require temperatures of around 25°C and a relative humidity of at least 50 per cent, preferably higher. Under hot, dry conditions they will refuse to feed and quickly die.

Geckos from Africa include several in the genus *Pachydactylus*, of which Bibron's gecko, *P. bibronii* is the largest and most common. This species and its close relatives have expanded toe-discs and camouflaged coloration. Most of them come from arid environments and can be treated in the same way as the *Hemidactylus* and *Tarentola* species mentioned above, as can another widespread southern African species, Wahlberg's velvet gecko, *Homopholis wahlbergii*. All these species adapt well to captivity and breed readily and regularly, although they have received little attention from lizard-keepers so far.

21.   Several small Asian geckos are attractive and are quite easy to care for once their requirements are understood. This is *Cyrtodactylus pinguensis*.

2: SMALL DESERT GECKOS

A large number of small geckos live in desert regions throughout the world. Many of these are highly adapted to an arid environment and their specialisations make them of great interest to herpetologists. They often show great parallelism in their body shapes and colours, so that 'suites' of species from North Africa and Australia, for instance, often look alike. Although a large proportion of them, for instance those hailing from Australia, are not freely available, those which have found their way into captivity have proven to be fairly easily catered for.

Because their lifestyles are somewhat similar to the eublepharid geckos described in the previous chapter, their care in captivity is also similar. Most of these species are unable to climb to any great extent and open cages are often feasible provided that their chosen food is not able to escape. Excessively high temperatures are not necessary – in nature, these species are crepuscular and/or nocturnal and only venture out on to the surface when temperatures have dropped. During the day they mostly live in deep burrows where the temperature is moderate and where a certain amount of moisture is

22.   Velvet gecko, *Homopholis wahlbergii*, a chunky South African species.

retained. Their preferred temperature seems to be approximately 25–30°C and the best arrangement is to heat their cages from below, using equipment which provides a gentle but even heat. This should be positioned under about half of the cage so that a range of temperatures is available. Alternatively, a spotlight can be used to heat one part of the cage, in which case, although the geckos will not bask directly, they will have the opportunity to absorb heat from the warmer patch of sand which retains heat after the spotlight is switched off.

Cage substrate for lizards of this type should be free-running sand or very fine, rounded pebbles of quartz or a similar material – the geckos' colours tend to reflect the type of sand on which they are naturally found, and an attempt to simulate this will enhance the set-up. Larger rocks or pebbles can be scattered over the surface, and a number of the more dwarf succulent plants are suitable and attractive additions. The geckos must have a secure place in which to hide during the day and this can consist of a piece of curved bark or a small pile of rocks. Alternatively, an upturned clay or plastic box with a small entrance hole will serve very well. The sand under and around the retreat should be sprayed regularly so that the geckos can shed their skins easily and this simple technique will go a long way towards maintaining them in good condition. In addition, many species seem unable to drink from a water bowl and regular spraying is especially important for them.

All these geckos are insectivorous. They often seem rather inefficient in their hunting methods and active prey such as crickets can avoid them quite easily. If such food items are to be used they can be chilled in a refrigerator immediately before feeding, or partially disabled by clipping off parts of their legs. Furthermore, if the crickets are placed in a smooth-sided bowl they will be less likely to escape and this will increase the chances of the geckos finding them and also provide a good indication that an adequate number are being eaten. Every feed should be fortified by sprinkling a vitamin and mineral powder over the insects: a mixture of multivitamin powder mixed with an equal quantity of calcium carbonate seems to work well although females which have eggs developing may require more calcium. This can be provided by increasing the proportion of calcium carbonate in the supplementary powder, or by placing a dish containing small shavings of cuttlefish bone in the cage.

Sexing geckos of this type is fairly straightforward: males have a hemipenal sac immediately behind the cloaca, which shows as a slight swelling, sometimes paired, at the base of the tail. Mature males also tend to be more heavily built, especially in the neck and jaw regions. Males cannot normally be housed together without stressful fighting. One, two or three females can be housed together with a single male, however, and this is usually the best arrangement for breeding. If there are more females than this it is difficult to keep track of their feeding behaviour and one animal can easily become deprived of food by other, bolder ones. All the species in this category lay their eggs in pairs, although young females laying for the first time may lay but a single egg. The eggs are calcareous and may be stuck to each other and to the substrate they are laid in, or they may be loose. Females always bury their eggs in a moist substrate and this should be provided by introducing a small container of moist sand, sand and peat, or sand and sphagnum moss into the cage. It is helpful if this is partially covered, i.e. by cutting a small entrance hole in the lid rather than leaving the lid off altogether, and must be inspected daily, not only to check for eggs but also to renew the substrate if it begins to dry out. Once the eggs are found, they can remain in the egg-laying substrate or, more effectively, placed in moist vermiculite in a suitable container. This can consist of a small plastic food container, half-filled with the chosen substrate, moistened with about one-third its volume of water, and placed in an incubator. The lid of the container should be ventilated with a few tiny holes and labelled with the date of laying as well as any other relevant information. The eggs require a temperature of about 30°C but, as these species probably all have temperature dependent sex determination, some experimentation will be required in order to obtain the sex ratios required; these data are not yet available as none of the species have been produced in sufficient numbers for the results to be conclusive. These geckos tend to be less prolific than typical geckos; every effort should be made to hatch any eggs produced.

Rearing the young should not present any problems save that of obtaining a sufficient quantity of small insect prey – young crickets are the most convenient but an attempt should be made to vary this with other species such as small waxworms. Vitamin and mineral supplements, as described for the adults, are essential. They should be kept singly, or in small groups of similar-sized individuals, in small plastic boxes, where their progress can be more easily monitored. Cage embellishments should be kept to a minimum, a small piece of bark resting on the sand being quite sufficient. One end of the box should be lightly sprayed regularly, every other day if possible, as the young geckos may take some time before they learn to drink from a water bowl. Many of the smaller species will mature and begin breeding in less than one year.

Representative species

Some of the most fascinating desert geckos are Australian and belong to the genus *Nephrurus*. These are short, squat lizards with huge heads, bulging eyes and short, often turnip-shaped tails. They adapt well to captivity but are, unfortunately, rarely available at present although a few captive-bred animals are being produced.

The casque-headed gecko, *Geckonia chazalae*, from North Africa, is very similar in appearance to the previous genus and is slightly more easily obtained. It inhabits the gravelly troughs between sand dunes and appears more at home on a substrate of small rocks and pebbles, although it will fare equally well on sand.

23.　One of the bizarre knob-tailed geckos from Australia, *Nephrurus laevissimus*.

24.　The helmeted gecko, *Geckonia chazalae*, is a strange species from North African desert regions which does very well in captivity.

Two species from the Namib Desert in southwest Africa are worth consideration although they are totally different in appearance and ecology. The Namib ground gecko, *Chondrodactylus angulifer*, is a large, heavily built species with a tuberculate skin. It is robust and aggressive, and will usually eat newborn mice once it attains a sufficient size. Males of this species will attack each other and may also attack females. For this reason they are normally kept separately except for mating, and any new introductions should be carefully supervised until a fairly harmonious pecking order is established.

The web-footed gecko, *Palmatagecko rangei*, is completely different. It has a slim, wraith-like body and spindly limbs. The toes of all four feet are joined by a web, which enables it to run across the fine, wind-blown sand of its native habitat. The most striking feature is the pair of large bulbous eyes, which are dark brown and red and stand out against the pinkish-brown colour of the head and back. The underside and legs are pure white. Although not often seen in captivity, the web-footed gecko appears to live well under the conditions described above. Its appearance is most dramatically set off by the use of fine, pale coloured sand, to look like its natural habitat. Small, soft-bodied insects and insect larvae appear to be its preferred prey.

The Asian desert geckos are separated taxonomically into a sub-family, the Teratoscincinae. To all intents and purposes, however, they can be treated in the same manner as other desert geckos. There are only three species, and they are all included in the genus *Teratoscincus*: *T. scincus*, *T. microlepis* and *T. przewalskii*. All species are brown or yellowish and have large overlapping scales. They have large bulbous

25.   The web-footed gecko, *Palmatagecko rangei*, a highly specialised desert species from Namibia.

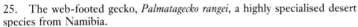

26. The Asian members of the genus *Teratoscincus* are attractive and popular lizards. Several forms are bred in captivity in small numbers.

eyes and are alert and attractive lizards with a great deal of 'personality'. Collectively, they range across the deserts, mountains and steppes of Central Asia, often occurring in dense colonies. They appear to be exclusively ground-dwelling, living in burrows during the day and emerging on to the surface of the sand or gravel at night to feed. One disconcerting habit is for nervous individuals to cast off large areas of their skin if they are held; handling should therefore be kept to a minimum, at least until established. Otherwise, their care and breeding is as described above. A pair of thin-shelled eggs is laid, buried in moist sand. These should be handled very gently, preferably with a small spoon, and incubated separately.

3: DAY GECKOS

Although a number of species of geckos are diurnal in their habitats, the species referred to here are those specifically called 'day geckos', that is, the species in the genus *Phelsuma*.

There is no doubt that these species are among the most colourful and popular of all lizards. Apart from their brilliant coloration, they usually adapt well to captivity, are engagingly active and often breed successfully with the minimum of special attention. A total of about twenty-three species are recognised, with their natural distribution centred on Madagascar and neighbouring Indian Ocean islands such as Mauritius and the Seychelles. Although there are a few dull-coloured members in the genus, the species that find their way into the reptile hobby are almost invariably those with bright green or blue-green colours, several of which are briefly described below. The care and breeding of the various species appears to be similar, although allowances must be made for differences in size. Certain species appear to adapt rather better than others, although there is no obvious reason why this should be so.

Day geckos are the perfect subjects for a natural or semi-natural set-up, even though they will fare equally well in a cage with newspaper as a substrate and very little in the way of fixtures and fittings. They spend the greater part of their time above ground level and so their cage should be at least 40 cm tall for the small species and 60 cm or more for the larger ones. They should also be provided with an abundance of vertical surfaces on which to perch, and these can be provided by fixing smooth branches, or lengths of thick bamboo, into the cage. Living plants with firm stems or trunks, such as *Yucca*, small palms, cycads and dragon trees (*Dracaena*) are even better. The cage should be well lit, especially if living plants are included, but also for the benefit of the lizards, and at least some of the light should originate from a natural spectrum fluorescent tube. Despite their tropical origins, day geckos are not sensitive to cool conditions and a background temperature of around 25°C seems to be adequate. They will often sit on top of a fluorescent tube if it is accessible and this serves as a 'hot-spot' should they require additional heat during the day; if the temperature drops slightly at night this will not cause any problems.

Similarly, although they appear to relish a thorough spraying of their cage, they will come to no harm if the atmosphere dries out for a day or two. The cage should not, in any case, be allowed to become continuously dripping wet. Conditions which are permanently too dry, on the other hand, may lead to problems in shedding, especially of the skin on their toes, leading to difficulty in climbing. The best arrangement (as with many lizards) is to provide plenty of ventilation but to spray the inside of the cage thoroughly once every day. If living plants are stood in their pots, their soil should be kept damp at all times and this will help by providing a small area which is always humid.

Day geckos are mainly insectivorous in their diet, taking all of the commonly used invertebrate food items such as crickets, locusts, waxworms, spiders and others. Variety is important if the animals are to be kept healthy. In addition, they will also lick the juice from over-ripe fruit and drink any sweet fluids such as honey or artificial nectar. A cocktail of fruit juice, honey, molasses, and fruit syrup and a liquid vitamin mixture, such as 'Abidec' has been used successfully by several zoos, but a simpler method of giving them extra vitamins, which seems to work just as well, is to place one or two drops of a sweet-tasting liquid vitamin preparation on to a sugar cube. The geckos will lick away at this until it is completely consumed, at which point it can be replaced with another cube. Other supplements which are essential to their well-being are powdered vitamin and mineral supplements, which should be added to every insect meal unless ultra-violet light is provided, and extra calcium for the females. The latter will accept fairly large pieces of cuttlefish bone if these are placed in a small dish, and will store the surplus in the special calcium sacs on either side of their throats.

All day geckos are highly territorial, including, to some extent, the females. For this reason they require spacious cages with plenty of perches and it may be necessary to remove stressed or damaged animals at short notice. Even juveniles will rarely tolerate other individuals of the same species in close proximity, which can make rearing them a time-consuming business since each one needs a separate cage and individual attention.

Breeding takes place regularly once a compatible pair or group is established. Mature males can be distinguished by the presence of pre-anal pores and the obvious hemipenal bulges at the base of their tails, while females soon develop large calcium sacs once they have been given an opportunity to ingest this mineral (newly imported females rarely show signs of these sacs). Females which are about to lay eggs are easily spotted as two large white patches form in their abdomen. There should be no need to handle the geckos in order to check any of the above conditions as it is easier, and less stressful, to encourage them on to the glass front or sides of the cage. The females lay their eggs in a secluded part of the cage, often returning to the same place each time. A pair of eggs may be produced by each female every four or five weeks over an extended breeding season (usually the spring and summer). If possible, the eggs should be removed from the cage and incubated artificially. To do this, they are simply placed in a small plastic box with a layer of sand or pea-gravel on the bottom to prevent them from rolling around. Occasionally, however, the eggs are attached to the sides of the cage, in which case it will be necessary to cover them with a small transparent container, firmly taped to the cage.

Although the eggs are hard-shelled and do not require to take up water during the incubation period, young day geckos may have trouble hatching successfully unless the environment around their egg is humid. This can be achieved by lightly spraying them each day towards the end of the incubation period, or by keeping a small piece of damp sponge or cotton-wool at one end of the box. They should be left in the same container until they have shed their skin, for which a high humidity is also required.

At a temperature of 28°C, the eggs normally hatch in five to six weeks, although the larger species may take longer, up to ten weeks. The sexes of the hatchlings will be determined by the temperature at which the eggs are incubated: low temperatures producing only females and high temperatures producing males. The critical temperature is not known for every species; some experimentation will therefore be necessary, but a good starting-point would appear to be 25–27°C for females and 29–31°C for males.

Because the hatchlings must be reared individually, they can be housed in small plastic boxes, supplied with a small dish of water and a fragment of bark under which to hide. They should be fed every day on newly hatched crickets or fruit flies, liberally dusted with a multi-vitamin/mineral powder. Even when vitamins are added to the diet, the young grow more quickly and develop better coloration if they are given access to ultra-violet light. This can be achieved by removing a panel from the top of the plastic box and replacing it with nylon mesh. The boxes are then lined up on a shelf over which a suitable fluorescent light is suspended. The distance from the light to the tops of the cages should be as small as possible, certainly no more than 30 cm, for the method to be effective, and the geckos must have the opportunity to hide from the light if they so wish. Under these conditions, growth is rapid and the smaller species will be half-grown in three to four months. At this stage they require larger accommodation, similar to that described for the adults, and pieces of egg-shell or cuttlefish bone can be provided for the females. Sexual maturity is attained in about one year or slightly less for the smaller species, but takes rather longer, eighteen months to two years, for the larger ones.

Problems encountered during rearing can usually be put down to nutritional inadequacies. These may take three forms: skeletal deformities, often involving the spine; paralysis of the hind legs, often following a fall; and convulsions, usually associated with handling or fighting. These problems can affect all stages of captive-bred geckos from newly hatched individuals right up to young adults. There is no sure way of avoiding them, although plenty of ultra-violet, preferably via a powerful source such as a blacklight fluorescent tube, coupled with a varied diet will go a long way towards eliminating them.

Representative species

Although the larger species of *Phelsuma* make spectacular exhibits, several of the smaller ones adapt better to close confinement and tend to look more 'at home' in a typical vivarium set-up. One of the best

27. The flat-tailed day gecko, *Phelsuma laticauda*, possible the easiest of the small day geckos.

species is undoubtedly *P. laticauda*, sometimes known as the flat-tailed day gecko. This species is brilliant green with three prominent, red, tear-drop markings on the dorsal surface. The neck is dusted with bright yellow or gold scales, several red bands cross the top of the head

28. *Phelsuma lineatus* is another attractive species of small day gecko.

and snout and the rims of the eyes are bright blue. This species grows to about 12 cm and has a fairly calm temperament, soon recognising possible sources of food and waiting eagerly for the cage to be opened. It breeds readily in captivity, each female laying a pair of eggs every four to five weeks during the spring and summer if adequately fed. *P. cepediana* is slightly larger and predominantly blue in colour with red markings. This species adapts less readily, in my experience, and may require rather more humid conditions than the other species: its eggs are unlikely to hatch unless they are also kept in a humid environment. *P. lineatus* is larger still, growing to about 15 cm in total length and has a deep green back with a large red blotch in the centre. A dark line runs from the angle of the jaws, right along the flanks and on to the base of the tail, and the underside is yellow, fading to white on the chin and throat. The upper surface of the tail is brilliant turquoise. This species can be kept under the same conditions as *P. laticauda* and, although it is not so widely bred in captivity, its breeding requirements are probably similar and equally easy to provide. Probably the easiest of all species to keep and breed is *P. dubia*. Unfortunately, this robust species is not nearly as colourful as many of the others, being dull olive-green all over. Females lay eggs repeatedly throughout the year.

Many other small day geckos may be available from time to time. As far as is known, they all require the same conditions as those described above. All are worth considering as potential subjects for vivarium culture.

Of the larger species, *Phelsuma madagascariensis, P. standingi*, and *P. sundbergi* are available from time to time but are invariably expensive. These are all large, bright green geckos, although *P. standingi* is more bluish than the others, which tend to be bright green or yellowish green. *P. madagascariensis* has, in addition, orange bands across the head and body, more noticeable in juveniles, which also have bright orange beneath their tails. A fourth large species, *P. guentheri*, is an endangered species from Round Island and is successfully bred in several zoos. This is not a colourful species, however, being dull brown with scattered darker blotches. The hatchlings are pale grey.

All these species grow to a total length of 20–25 cm, and the males are generally larger and more colourful than females. Sexing is still most reliably carried out, however, by examining them for the presence of pre-anal pores (males) or calcium sacs (females) as in the case of the smaller species. Males and females of these species are also highly territorial and it is usually only practicable to keep them in single pairs.

29. The eggs of day geckos are hard-shelled, rounded and usually lightly adhesive. The hatchlings are not as brightly coloured as the adults and are quite easily reared.

They require very large cages, at least one metre high if possible. Thick, vertical perches are preferred, the trunks of living or dead *Yucca* or palms being ideal, and closely approximating to their natural habitat. A temperature of about 25°C is satisfactory, and ultra-violet light is essential. Although these larger species are also insectivorous, larger prey can be offered, and some will accept newborn mice. They also relish chopped soft fruit, jam and honey and these are good vehicles for adding the necessary vitamin and mineral supplements. They have been observed eating pieces of gravel from the substrate of their cage; this appears to be intentional and should not give cause for concern.

Females will lay several clutches of paired eggs during the course of the breeding season, which usually extends from early spring to late summer. There is a very real danger of them becoming calcium deficient, however, unless plenty of calcium is given, in addition to the vitamin D3 provided by exposure to the ultra-violet light. A deficiency will result in poorly formed eggs, laid without shells in extreme cases, and poor hatching results. If this situation continues, the females will sequester calcium from their skeletons, leading to deformities and an early death. There is, therefore, a strong case for separating the male and female after one or two clutches have been laid in order for the female to replenish her reserves. Since they are long-lived there is little point in forcing more young per season than can be produced without detrimental effects on the health of the female.

The eggs are stuck to one another and usually hidden in a hollow tube or amongst leaves and should be removed to be incubated separately. There is no need for these to be kept under humid conditions. At a temperature of 29–30°C, they hatch in about seven weeks, although there appears to be some variation, both between species and within species. This temperature appears to produce mostly males – in order to produce females the incubation temperature should be lower, in which case the eggs will take longer to hatch.

4: SPHAERODACTYLINE GECKOS

This group of geckos, with such an alarming name, represents an interesting off-shoot of the gecko family and consists of a relatively small number of exclusively American species. Most are tropical, although some range into sub-tropical regions, e.g. southern Florida, and they are usually found on the ground or in low vegetation in shady overgrown places. They are characterised by a small body size, mainly diurnal activity pattern and clutches consisting of but a single egg.

Many of them are brightly coloured and they are especially suited to a well-planted vivarium, where a colony of individuals or even a mixed collection of two or more species will thrive and breed with the minimum of maintenance.

A large cage is best if a number of animals are to be housed together. This should have a layer of drainage material, covered by leaf-litter or a mixture of peat and small bark chippings. Plants can be planted directly into this substrate or left in their pots. Epiphytic plants such as orchids and small bromeliads, attached to dead branches or pieces of driftwood, are especially suitable. If running water can be arranged so much the better but, failing this, the cage should be thoroughly sprayed daily, both for the benefit of the plants and also for the lizards which seem to prefer a high relative humidity. Ventilation, however, should be good, so that stagnant air does not accumulate in the cage. An even temperature of about 25°C should be provided throughout the cage, although a reduced 'hot-spot' produced by a low wattage spotlight or by a fluorescent tube, will be useful. Adequate lighting should, in any case, be provided, with preferably a tube giving ultra-violet (for the lizards) and another producing a warmer light (for the plants).

All species are insectivorous, but their size obviously limits them to small insects such as young crickets and waxworms, house flies and

30.   Sexual dimorphism in *Gonatodes vittatus*. The male is above the female.

sweepings from which the larger items have been removed. Dusting the food with a vitamin and mineral supplement would seem to be a good idea, and the inclusion of a natural spectrum light in the cage would also help with vitamin production. Females should have access to extra calcium, either sprinkled over the food as a fine powder or placed separately in the cage in the form of crushed egg-shell or cuttlefish bone.

In most species the males are readily identified by their brighter coloration, and in several species, such as *Gonatodes vittatus*, they are so unlike the females that they may be mistaken for separate species. Both males and females are territorial to some extent, although in a large enough cage it should be possible to maintain a small colony of individuals which will each take over a proportion of the cage as their exclusive territory. In this way social interactions between males, as well as between males and females, can be observed.

Breeding takes place over a prolonged season, usually spring and summer unless the temperature and light-cycle are artificially manipulated. The females lay their single, hard-shelled eggs every three to four weeks, hiding them behind bark, beneath a plant pot or in some other crevice. Several females will often choose the same site for laying, and caches of eggs may be found. The eggs are smooth and are only lightly stuck to the substrate, or they may be completely free.

103

They are about the size of a pea. Under normal circumstances, the eggs should be removed when they are discovered and incubated separately. They take between two and three months to hatch when kept at a temperature of 28°C. It is not known whether or not the species in this sub-family show temperature dependent sex determination, although it seems likely. The newly hatched young are very tiny, but will readily take very small crickets. In many species, they are coloured differently to the adults, and are often more striking in appearance. They grow quickly if adequately fed and mature within one year.

Representative species

Although there is not a big demand for these small geckos, being of interest mainly to specialists, members of at least two genera are imported occasionally, and several species are bred regularly in captivity. Three species of *Sphaerodactylus* occur in Florida, although two of them are introductions there. The ashy gecko, *S. cinereus*, is the most common: it is native to Cuba and Hispaniola. Adults are tan coloured, densely covered with dark brown reticulations. The juveniles, by contrast, are grey with distinct dark crossbands and a red tail. Other species of *Sphaerodactylus* are found throughout the West Indies.

31.   Ashy gecko, *Sphaerodactylus cinereus*, a small West Indian species introduced into Florida.

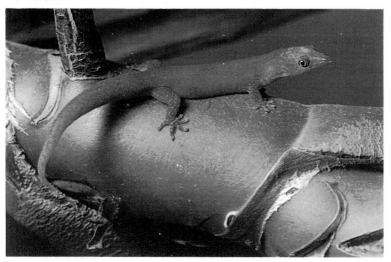

Members of the genus *Gonatodes* tend to be slightly larger and more robust in appearance. The yellow-headed gecko, *G. albogularis*, is another Florida immigrant and is native to several of the larger West Indian islands as well as parts of the Central and South American mainland. Males are dark bluish grey with a yellow-brown head, whereas the females and juveniles are mottled brown all over. A number of other species are found on the West Indian islands and on parts of the neighbouring mainland. These include the striped gonatodes, *G. vittatus*, mentioned above in connection with its sexual dimorphism. Males are tan coloured with a broad and prominent black-edged, chalky white stripe starting on the snout and passing right down the back on to the tail; females are pale brown with dark blotches and the dorsal stripe is only faintly represented. Juveniles are similar to the females. *G. ceciliae* is rather larger and both sexes are dark in colour, almost black. The male, however, has a large bright red patch just behind the head.

5: DIPLODACTYLINE GECKOS

The final section of the gecko family consists of the members of the sub-family Diplodactylinae. These geckos are found only in Australia, New Zealand and New Caledonia and, as such, are rarely available to enthusiasts in Europe and North America. They are so interesting, however, that a brief note on their care and breeding is considered worthwhile.

The Australian species are found throughout a wide range of habitats. Many of them, such as the *Oedura* and *Diplodactylus* species, live in semi-arid habitats, often under the bark of dead trees or in rock crevices. These species can be treated in much the same way as the small desert geckos described previously, but with two important differences. The *Oedura* species will feel more secure, and therefore fare better, if they are able to retreat into a tight space, with their bodies in contact with as many surfaces as possible. This can be achieved by making stacks of bark or wafers of rock (such as slate) and wiring them together securely. In this way, cracks of varying widths will be created and each gecko will be able to find the size into which it best fits. The most common species of *Oedura*, *O. castelnaui*, will use either rock or bark crevices but other species are more specific and will prefer one or the other. Both types of retreat should be provided if there is any doubt. The most common species of *Diplodactylus*, *D. ciliaris*, however, will not hide away in this manner but will rest by lying along a piece of dead branch and relying on its camouflage to escape notice.

32. *Oedura castelnaui* is among the more commonly bred Australian velvet geckos. This example is a mutant in which the dark pigmentation is absent.

33. The grey form of the Australian spiny-tailed gecko, *Diplodactylus ciliaris*.

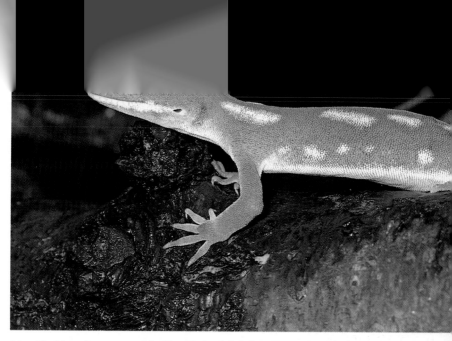

34. *Naultinus elegans*, one of the New Zealand diplodactyline geckos which gives birth to live young.

35. One of the large and attractive diplodactyline geckos from New Caledonia, *Rhacodactylus auriculatus*.

Other similar species may have different requirements and some experimentation will be necessary.

Oedura are velvety-skinned geckos with a flattened tail. They grow to about 15 cm in length, of which one-third to a half consists of the tail. *O. castelnaui* is elegantly banded in dark brown and tan, and a much paler mutation has arisen from captive-bred stock. Other species in the genus are of similar coloration but their markings may consist of spots, blotches or reticulations. *Diplodactylus ciliaris* is smaller, growing to about 12 cm in length, and is more slender. It is highly variable in colour and several races are recognised; it may be silvery grey with hardly any trace of markings, to brick red with patches of white, orange or ochre. Other species in this genus include the remarkable golden-tailed gecko, *D. taenicauda*, which has an overall coloration consisting of black with a network of white reticulations, save for the tail, which has a bright orange stripe along its upper surface. The eyes of both these *Diplodactylus* species are bright orange with a complicated pattern of white squiggles.

These species, like all the other Australian diplodatyline geckos, and most of the species from New Caledonia, lay soft-shelled eggs, and gravid females must be given a container of moist sand for laying. Pairs of eggs are laid throughout the spring and summer and each female will lay every four or five weeks if she is kept in good condition. The eggs must be removed from the cage and incubated in moist vermiculite in the same way as those of the leopard gecko and other eublepharids (Chapter 9). At a temperature of 28°C the eggs will hatch in 55–60 days. It is not known whether these species have temperature dependent sex determination.

Two genera of geckos from New Zealand, *Naultinus* and *Hoplodactylus*, are almost unique in their family by giving birth to live young. They produce only one litter each year, and their gestation periods are long, almost twelve months in some species. These species should be kept permanently in pairs or small breeding groups. The males are not so territorial as in other geckos and it is sometimes possible to keep them together, with caution. The *Naultinus* species are bright green in colour, diurnal, arboreal and have prehensile tails. They should be given plenty of branches and twigs to climb among. Living plants are better than dead branches because the geckos can then hide among the leaves, as they would in the wild. The *Hoplodactylus* species, on the other hand, are mostly drab in colour, nocturnal and live on the ground or on tree trunks. Cages for these species should be arranged accordingly. All the New Zealand species require a moderate temperature, 20–25°C at most, and a definite cooler winter period if they are to breed. They may be kept outside in aviaries in areas where the local climate is not too severe. All are insectivorous and will take crickets, waxworms and so on, with vitamin and mineral supplements. A blacklight would appear to be a worthwhile accessory, at least for the diurnal species, but reliable information is lacking.

The New Caledonian species are placed in the genus *Rhacodactylus*. One species, *R. trachyrhynchus* , gives birth to live young but the others lay soft-shelled eggs, as far as is known. *R. auriculatus* and *R. chahoua* have been bred in captivity. Both species grow quite large, up to 30 cm at least. Although they are arboreal, they inhabit areas with low humidity, so they require large cages with plenty of vertically arranged branches and logs, a dry substrate of gravel, sand or dry leaves and only occasional spraying. They are a pleasure to keep, being of calm temperament and will, in time, learn to accept food from the hand. Unfortunately, they are not bred in large numbers and are fully protected in their places of origin. For these reasons they are not likely to be freely available for some time yet but if they can be obtained they should be treasured.

Other diplodactyline geckos may become available in time. All would make superb subjects for the vivarium provided they are looked after carefully and their requirements researched and provided for conscientiously. Most of these geckos are not prolific breeders, even in the wild, and should not be thought of as expendable 'pets' but as precious creatures which should be propagated and selectively distributed to other interested enthusiasts.

CHAPTER 11

Snake Lizards

The snake lizards, or pygopods, are exclusively Australasian in origin and, as such, are rarely available to the pet trade outside that continent. This is rather a pity, as the few which have found their way into private collections have proven to be interesting and attractive animals which would almost certainly adapt well and possibly breed readily, given the numbers required for this to be possible.

The thirty-odd species are all slender, elongated and without legs, but vestigial hind limbs are present in the form of small, scaly flaps. They also lack functional eyelids, like snakes and geckos, and the scale covering the eye is shed along with the rest of the skin. Of the species so far studied, all lay a pair of soft-shelled eggs and all vocalise. With the obvious exception of their lack of limbs, they parallel the geckos in many ways and are thought to have originated from the same ancestral stock. Little is known of their natural history, and several are known from only a small sample of specimens.

The small amount of information which is available suggests that the larger species at least are easily cared for. They require moderate temperatures, about 25–30°C being suitable, and a dry substrate of sand or gravel. Pieces of bark, flat rocks or large dried leaves can be used to provide cover and most species will burrow, given the chance. Further information on their requirements outside their natural range, especially in respect of reproduction, is sadly lacking and unlikely to become available until the laws which prevent their exportation are relaxed.

The most familiar species is probably *Lialis burtoni*, Burton's snake lizard, one of the largest at 60 cm, and one of the most unusual. This species has a greatly elongated and pointed snout and occurs in a variety of colour forms, the most common of which are plain cream or dark brown. Some specimens have stripes and/or spots along their flanks. This species apparently feeds mainly on other lizards, especially

36. Flap-footed lizards are rarely seen in captivity. This species, *Pygopus lepidopodus* seems to be one of the easiest to keep, being larger than most and willing to eat common insects.

small skinks and geckos, which are common in the arid regions it inhabits, and for this reason it would be the least valuable as a vivarium subject. The genus *Pygopus* consists of two species which, between them, cover the whole of Australia. Both are large, growing to about 60 cm in total length. Both are insectivorous and have been successfully kept in captivity over a long period of time. Of the other species, almost nothing is known that would have a bearing on their care in captivity.

CHAPTER 12

Night Lizards

The night lizards form a small family, Xantusiidae, consisting of only sixteen species. These are characterised by having fused eyelids, plate-like scales on the back and head and small, granular scales on the flanks and underside. They are found in specialised habitats in North and Central America and the West Indies, and are mostly small and have dingy coloration. All give birth to small litters of live young.

Only two species are likely to be seen in captivity, both North American. The desert night lizard, *Xantusia vigilis*, has a maximum length of about 8 cm, of which half is tail. It is pale brown, tan or pinkish in colour, suffused with black flecks. It occurs in desert and semi-desert areas and is commonly associated with *Yucca* and *Agave* plants, typically hiding amongst the dead-leaf-sheaths at the base of the plants. *X. henshawi*, the granite night lizard, is somewhat larger, growing to 12 cm in total length, and rather more attractive, with large, deep brown blotches over a yellowish background. This species is greatly flattened, an adaptation to its habit of hiding behind large flakes of exfoliating granite. Like *X. vigilis*, it is also found in desert regions, but is restricted to rock outcrops.

Both these species will live for a long time under the most basic conditions. They require a dry substrate of sand and pieces of flat rock beneath or between which they will spend much of their time. A constant temperature of 23–28° C has proved to be suitable over an extended period, and this is most conveniently provided by an underfloor heat system. Both are insectivorous and will take small crickets, locusts and waxworms, etc. Both species can be kept together in a community set-up. There is no reliable way of telling the sexes apart, and captive breeding has not been recorded.

It is suggested that either of these two species would make ideal subjects for a natural type of vivarium, with sand and rock fragments forming the base, and a jumble of larger rocks providing cover for the

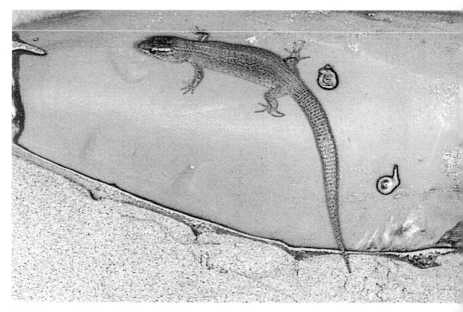

37.   Desert night lizard, *Xantusia vigilis*, a small and common species which would be well-suited to a natural desert set-up.

38.   The granite night lizard, *Xantusia henshawi*, is probably the most attractive member of the family Xantusiidae.

lizards. Many species of common cacti and succulents, such as *Agave*, *Opuntia*, *Echeveria* and *Dudleya* are found in the same part of the world as the night lizards and small specimens of any of these would thrive under the conditions favoured by the lizards, with the addition of a suitable light source, which should be bright.

113

CHAPTER 13

Iguanas

The family Iguanidae consists of well over 600 species, many of which have attracted the attention of lizard-keepers owing to their bright coloration and diurnal activity pattern. In many species the males are easily distinguished from the females by virtue of their brighter colours and dorsal crests, dewlaps or other ornamentation. For this reason, beginners often fall into the trap of selecting only males and ignoring the females, which are dull by comparison.

Iguanas of some description are found virtually throughout the North and South American continents, save only the cold regions in the far north and south, and the very highest mountain ranges. In the West Indian islands, speciation has run riot, with each island harbouring a range of endemic species and subspecies, especially within the enormous genus *Anolis*, of which over 100 species are recognised. Exact identification of many of these can be difficult (if not impossible) unless their origin is documented. Other large genera include the swifts, or spiny lizards, genus *Sceloporus* from North and Central America and the lava lizards, genus *Liolaemus*, from South America (sometimes also known as Chilean swifts, despite their occurrence in neighbouring countries). An additional seven species of iguanids occur on the Island of Madagascar and another three on the Fijian and Tongan Islands.

Of the larger species, the genus *Iguana* is by far the best known for it contains the well-known common or green iguana, an attractive and popular exhibit in zoos as well as a perpetual standby for the pet trade. Other large species are found in the genera *Sauromalus*, the chuckwallas, and *Ctenosaura*, the spiny-tailed iguanas, among others. Specialised groups of large species, which are unlikely to come the way of any but the more wealthy collectors include the species from the Galapagos, most notably the marine iguana, *Amblyrhychus cristatus*, the *Brachylophus* species from Fiji and Tonga and the West Indian ground

39.   The common iguana, *Iguana iguana*, is a well-known and popular 'pet'.

iguanas of the genus *Cyclura*. All of this latter group of species are considered endangered and are strictly protected by international law.

Not only do the size and appearance of iguanas vary, but also their feeding habits, habitat preferences and behaviour patterns. Because of this, it is not possible to give any generalised information on their care and breeding and they have been sub-divided into two groups so that they can be dealt with more logically.

1: THE COMMON IGUANA AND OTHER LARGE HERBIVOROUS SPECIES

The requirements for species in this group are based on those of the common iguana, *I. iguana*, which is by far the best known. This and similar species require very large cages, ideally room-sized, or the freedom to wander throughout a room or conservatory for at least part of each day. Although juveniles can be housed in conventional vivaria, these are soon outgrown and the close confinement of adults is unsatisfactory. This consideration must be uppermost *before* small specimens are purchased.

The common iguana hails from Central and South America, where it is found in a variety of habitats from semi-desert to tropical rainforest. It is typically found, however, close to rivers, often resting on boughs which hang out over the water, ready to drop off and swim to safety if it feels under threat. It varies from green to bluish grey in coloration and specimens from some parts of the range may have orange flanks. The tail is marked with broad black bands. Adults have a dorsal crest of long tooth-like scales and scaly folds of skin around their throats. The subspecies *Iguana iguana rhinoceros* also has a small horn-like scale on the tip of its snout, and this form is sometimes sold erroneously as the 'rhinoceros' iguana (a totally different species).

These iguanas are imported in huge quantities for the pet trade and, although they often fall into the wrong hands, they can, with the right amount of dedication, make spectacular and responsive pets. The hatchings measure about 25 cm in total length and can be kept in a cage measuring about one metre in length and half a metre in width and height. This should have a substrate of newspaper or gravel – if newspaper is used a small bowl of pea-gravel should also be included as the ingestion of small stones may be an essential aid to their digestion. Attempts to replicate their natural habitat by including living plants in the cage are usually doomed to failure – if the heat produced by the spotlight fails to dry them out, they will often be eaten by the iguanas. Young iguanas are especially sensitive to cool conditions and heating for their cage must be reliable and accurately controlled. The best arrangement is to heat the whole of the cage to a background temperature of 25°C by means of a heat pad, placed under the cage and controlled by a thermostat, and to boost this during the day with a fairly powerful spotlight aimed towards one end of the cage. A branch or shelf is arranged immediately beneath this spotlight so that the lizards can rapidly raise their body temperatures to at least 35°C. If necessary, the spotlight can also be controlled by a thermostat which will prevent overheating. This thermostat should be situated in the coolest part of the cage and set to switch the spotlight off if the temperature here rises above 30°C. In addition to the spotlight, a fluorescent ultra-violet light source should be installed above the basking area, one of the blacklight variety being preferred. A large bowl of water should be present at all times and the water should be changed daily.

Young iguanas will eat a certain amount of animal material in addition to vegetation. Crickets, waxworms and other insects can be added to the regular menu of chopped leaves, fruit and vegetables, and the whole should be generously sprinkled with a dietary supplement consisting of a proprietary multivitamin/mineral powder with added

116

calcium and vitamin D3. Juveniles are sometimes reluctant to begin feeding voluntarily and will often respond to hand feeding, when an item of food is placed in their mouths while they are lightly held.

With adequate care, the young iguanas will grow rapidly. As this occurs, they must be moved to progressively larger cages. These should be arranged in a similar fashion to that of the juveniles, but height is of special importance as they like to climb; in particular, adult males will invariably perch at the highest possible level, coming down to the ground only to eat and drink. Since adults can attain a total length of two metres, any branches or artificial perches in the cage must be of substantial material and firmly fixed to the floor and/or sides. Similarly, the water container must be large, although they rarely bathe provided they have access to clean drinking water and their cage is sprayed occasionally. If their food is washed and placed in the cage before it has had time to dry out completely, this will also contribute towards their water requirements.

Access to a warm basking area and to ultra-violet is just as important to the adults as it is to the juveniles. Animals which are deprived of these conditions lose their appetites, become dull and may eventually develop clinical symptoms such as hind-leg paralysis. In warm, sunny weather, the iguanas may be placed outside, either in an enclosure of wire or at liberty to bask in the open (under supervision). Under these conditions their coloration will improve dramatically and their behaviour will become more natural.

Breeding in captivity, outside their natural range, is rarely achieved and the young animals in the pet trade are invariably wild-caught or farmed on a large scale in their country of origin. Space and the associated territorial constraints are probably one of the major factors acting against captive breeding.

Adult males are easily distinguished from females by the much more prominent dorsal crest and the folded dewlaps which hang down from their throats. It is not possible to determine the sexes of hatchlings. Males are highly territorial and can only be kept one to a cage. They show characteristic head-bobbing behaviour directed not only at other males but also at females, lizards of other species and, often, their keeper. These are territorial displays and occur at all times of the year. Females tend not to be so violently territorial although a dominance hierarchy will usually be established if more than one is kept in a cage. Although they also head-bob to some extent, their displays are less vigorous. Mating takes place during the winter (in the northern hemisphere at least) and the eggs are laid in early spring. Between twenty and forty eggs constitute a normal clutch, and these are buried in sand; a suitable container must be placed in the cage well before egg-laying is expected because females like to dig exploratory holes before the actual nesting takes place. Once the eggs have been laid they should be removed from the sand and placed in damp vermiculite, as described in Chapter 7. The eggs should be incubated at 28–32°C, at which temperature they will hatch after a period of 60–80 days. The hatchlings should be removed from the incubator as soon as they have absorbed their yolk sacs, and housing and feeding are as described above.

There is some suggestion that in wild populations young iguanas eat the faeces of adults and that by doing so they inoculate their digestive systems with the bacteria which aid in the breaking down of vegetable matter. Experiments have shown that young which are not given the opportunity to do this grow more slowly and are more prone to nutritional deficiencies than those that are. This interesting aspect could easily be explored in a captive environment and possibly applied to other herbivorous species of lizards.

Other large herbivorous iguanas which are occasionally kept in captivity include the West Indian rhinoceros iguanas, *Cyclura cornuta*, as well as other members of the genus *Cyclura*. All these species are in imminent danger of extinction due to habitat destruction by human activities, including the release of goats, pigs, dogs and cats on the islands on which they live. They are all, therefore, completely protected under the Convention on International Trade in Endangered Species (CITES) and unlikely to be seen in captivity except in well-known zoological gardens and institutes. These huge, prehistoric-looking lizards adapt well to captivity, feeding for the most part on mixed vegetation of almost any sort, supplemented by a small proportion of animal material. Unfortunately, they appear to be very reluctant to breed in a captive environment unless they are maintained in spacious outdoor enclosures with access to unlimited sunshine.

The iguanas from the Fiji and Tonga Islands belong to the genus *Brachylophus* and three species are recognised at present. They are more closely related to the iguanas found on the Galapagos Islands and the West Indian Islands than to the South American species. All three species are also totally protected, although they fare quite well in captivity and have even been bred and raised to maturity in several North American zoos.

The chuckwallas, genus *Sauromalus*, form a distinct group of large herbivorous iguanas found in the desert regions of North America. Seven species are recognised, but only one, *S. obesus*, is commonly seen in captivity. This species is the most northerly occurring, and can

40. *Left*: One of the most colourful large iguanids is *Brachylophus fasciatus* from Fiji; it is rare and protected and therefore unlikely to appear in the pet trade.

41. *Right*: Chuckwalla, *Sauromalus obesus*, a large herbivorous iguanid from North American deserts.

42. Juvenile *Sauromalus hispidus*, a species of chuckwalla from Mexico, which is occasionally bred in captivity.

119

be found in fairly large numbers in the Sonoran and Colorado Deserts. Members of this species (and presumably the others also) live in discrete colonies among large rocky outcrops and hillsides, rarely venturing far from the cracks and crevices into which they quickly retreat if disturbed. They are drab brown in colour, with traces of dark bands on the tail and lower back. Juveniles are more brightly coloured than adults and their body bands are much more obvious. Even well-fed animals have flaps of skin along their flanks and necks, and these only disappear when they puff themselves up in display or in order to wedge themselves firmly into their retreats. They grow to about 40 cm in total length, but may appear much larger due to their considerable bulk. Sexual maturity is apparently attained at about 30 cm.

Captive chuckwallas adapt well if their basic requirements are understood. These include a large cage (100 × 50 cm minimum), a substrate of sand or gravel and plenty of large rocks amongst which to hide. The rocks must be heavy and firmly planted on the floor of the cage, otherwise the lizards will excavate beneath them, often with dire consequences. These lizards thrive under the most extreme heat. The background temperature of the cage should rise to about 30°C during summer days, and a spotlight should be installed at one end to give a hot-spot of at least 45°C. A large flat rock, placed beneath the spotlight, will provide a basking surface and will, in addition, hold the heat long after the spotlight has been switched off, allowing the lizards to extend their period of activity in a natural way. Otherwise, the temperature can be allowed to drop at night, and winter temperatures, night and day, should be appreciably lower than those during the summer if it is hoped to breed them.

Ultra-violet radiation, provided by blacklights or natural spectrum fluorescent tubes, is essential for good health, and these should be situated over the basking rock and close enough to it for the lizards to receive sufficient and effective radiation – a distance of not more than 30 cm is recommended. Wild chuckwallas exist on the most austere of diets, relying on the tough leaves and stems of succulent shrubs found in the places they inhabit. Their diet in captivity should not, therefore, be too luxurious and should consist mainly of green leaves and stalks of cabbage etc., root vegetables, beans and peas, including their pods. Fruit can be given occasionally as a 'treat' as can insects such as locusts. Vitamin and mineral supplements as described for the common iguana should be sprinkled on the food at least every other day. Although they will lick water from their scales or from the sides of the vivarium if this is sprayed, chuckwallas rely almost entirely on their food as a source of water.

120

43.   The desert iguana, *Dipsosaurus dorsalis*, is a medium-sized desert species which feeds almost exclusively on vegetation.

Adult males are larger than females, and have thicker tails. They are invariably darker in coloration, especially during the breeding season, which occurs during the spring. Like other iguanids, they are territorial, and only a single male can be kept in a cage, although he can share this with several females in a harem arrangement. Courtship involves head-bobbing displays by the male. The female lays 5–15 eggs about six weeks after mating and normally buries these in a shallow burrow she constructs, often beneath a rock. Captive females will often use a bowl of damp sand for egg-laying but this should be placed in the cage well beforehand. At a temperature of 32°C the eggs hatch in about 70 days. The hatchlings are about 10 cm in total length and will eat the same diet as the adults, but more finely chopped. Vitamin and mineral supplements and access to a good source of ultra-violet are important factors bearing upon the successful rearing of the young.

Also from the desert regions of North America is the desert iguana, *Dipsosaurus dorsalis*. This species is rather smaller than the chuckwallas, reaching a size of about 35 cm in total length, of which the tail accounts for over half. This pretty lizard is pale grey above with a fine network of darker reticulations, fading to uniform grey on the

121

flanks and pure white beneath. Its requirements in captivity are similar to the above species, although it is not associated with rocks but retreats into burrows in the sand at night or if disturbed, and basks on top of sand ridges. In practice, however, its primary requirements are plenty of heat, plenty of ultra-violet light, vitamins and minerals and a diet of vegetation and fruit with occasional insects. Although it is smaller, its cage should be of a similar size to that recommended for the chuckwallas because it is rather more active. Although this species enters the pet trade occasionally, it is not bred to any great extent. As far as is known, males are territorial and mating takes place in the spring. A clutch of 3–8 eggs is laid, but details of the incubation period under captive conditions are lacking. This species would make an excellent subject for a large naturalistic set-up, although any plants included would need to be either extremely well protected, or artificial.

2: SMALL AND MEDIUM-SIZED IGUANAS

Although the iguana family is best known for the large and impressive species dealt with in the first section, it also contains some 600 or so small to medium-sized lizards, many of which are brightly coloured, interesting and well-suited to vivarium culture.

Care of these species depends to some extent on their size but several basic principles apply to them all. They are highly territorial species in which the males are often larger than the females, more brightly coloured and may have dorsal crests, dewlaps, frills and head ornamentation, all associated with display. Males can rarely be kept together except in the very largest of cages. These species are more or less exclusively carnivorous, taking a range of prey from insects to small mammals, birds and other lizards, depending again on their size. All like to bask, and their cages must be equipped with a spotlight and an ultra-violet fluorescent tube, as well as background heating. Many species can be kept in a natural or semi-natural environment, using sand, rocks, dead wood, living plants, etc., depending on their origins. Because this group of lizards is so diverse, additional information is given for each of the separate species discussed below.

Representative species

Many of the more spectacular species are rainforest inhabitants. These include the basilisks, genus *Basiliscus*, of which two species may be available from time to time. The back legs of these lizards are greatly elongated and they often raise their front legs from the ground when

44. The plumed basilisk, *Basiliscus plumifrons*, an attractive tropical iguanid.

running at speed. *B. plumifrons*, the plumed basilisk, is a green lizard growing to about 60 cm, of which about two-thirds is accounted for by the tail. Males of this species have a high crest arising from the back of their heads and a high dorsal crest along the back and the upper tail. Females lack these characteristics. The common basilisk, *B. basiliscus*, is of a similar size and is brown in colour. Although males are larger and more boldly marked, the dorsal crest is lacking. Females as well as males may be territorial in these species and subordinates may have to be removed if they become stressed or physically damaged.

Both these species require very large cages. As they are semi-arboreal, their cage should be high (preferably at least one metre) as well as long. It should be furnished with several large branches to allow the lizards to perch and bask well off the ground and it may be possible to include one or two large, robust living plants in order to provide hiding places for the lizards and to enhance the general appearance. Substrate can be gravel or bark chippings, and a large water bowl should be included. A temperature of 25–30°C should be maintained at all times, preferably by underfloor heating, but a spotlight placed above one of the branches should be switched on during the day in order to provide a hot-spot. An ultra-violet source should be installed and switched on for the same period as the spotlight. Although there is no need to manipulate the temperature or lighting on a seasonal

123

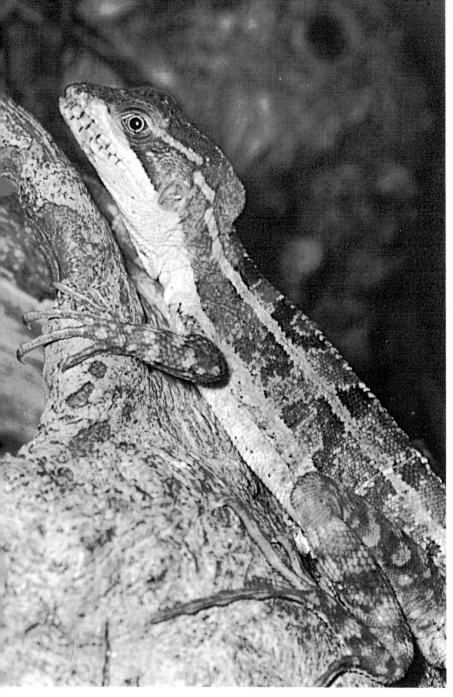

45. Brown basilisk, *Basiliscus basiliscus*, a species which is now bred in good numbers in several zoos and private collections.

basis, a small drop in temperature during the winter, together with shorter days, will not harm the lizards and may encourage breeding.

These species are almost entirely carnivorous and adults will take small mice as well as crickets, locusts, waxworms, etc. Hatchlings and juveniles will only take the smaller insects. Some individuals will also accept some vegetable material, such as tomatoes and other fruit. Each meal should be fortified with a vitamin and mineral supplement, and extra calcium may be necessary if breeding females are present.

Breeding appears to take place over an extended period and females may lay several clutches in the course of one breeding season. Clutches of 10–20 eggs are buried in a substrate of sand or peat, which should be placed in the cage for this purpose. Females often dig exploratory nests before the eggs are finally laid. The eggs should be removed for incubation in moist vermiculite and kept at a temperature of approximately 28–30°C, when they will hatch in 60–70 days.

The spindly hatchlings measure 10–15 cm in total length, and should be lively and agile. It is not possible to determine the sexes until they approach maturity at six to seven months of age. Provided they are strong and healthy when they hatch, they can be raised quite easily in a cage similar to that of the adults. They should be sprayed daily but ventilation should be good in order to prevent a stagnant atmosphere. A small group of hatchlings may be raised together without any problems but once sexual maturity is reached it is prudent to move or dispose of surplus males before fighting becomes a problem.

Other tropical and sub-tropical iguanids include the multitude of species placed in the genus *Anolis*. They are characterised by a narrow, pointed head, long legs and a long tail. Many are brightly coloured, usually some shade of green, but others are brown or brown and cream. Males invariably grow larger than females and have folded, fan-shaped dewlaps which they flick out when displaying. These dewlaps vary in colour according to species and this almost certainly serves to distinguish the various species where more than one occurs in the same area. Males will display to other males, females and to their own reflection!

Several of the species are large, approaching basilisks in size, and their care and maintenance is similar. The most common member of this group is *A. equestris*, the knight anole, a Cuban species which has been introduced into Florida. Other, more moderately sized *Anolis* include the common green anole, *A. carolinensis*, the Cuban anole, *A. sagrei*, and the large-headed anole, *A. cybotes*. The first of these is native to south eastern North America, but the others are all West Indian species which have become well-established in and around

46.   The helmeted iguana, *Corytophanes cristatus*, from South America, is a bizarre but interesting species which has bred in captivity on a few occasions.

47.   The knight anole, *Anolis equestris*, is one of the largest species in this huge genus.

48. *Left*: The green anole, *Anolis carolinensis*, one of the main standbys in the reptile trade.

49. *Right*: The Cuban anole, *Anolis sagrei*, introduced into Florida and now common there.

Florida and which have become common pet-trade items. Other species of *Anolis* are only likely to enter the reptile hobby in small numbers, but their care and breeding is likely to be similar.

All the smaller *Anolis* species lend themselves to a planted, naturalistic set-up, with living plants. Substrate can be gravel, bark chippings, dead leaves or a mixture of peat and chopped sphagnum. Small plants can be left in their pots and partially buried in the substrate and the anoles will climb about in the foliage as well as over the pots themselves, giving them a variety of perches and an opportunity to hide away. They require a background temperature of about 25°C and a hot-spot which reaches 35°C during the day. This should be directed at one corner of the cage only, and a few dead branches and twigs should be placed here so that the lizards can find a suitable basking place. An ultra-violet light should be installed in this part of the cage. The cage should be thoroughly sprayed daily as anoles are often reluctant to drink from a water bowl. A diet of crickets, small locusts, waxworms and, especially, sweepings of spiders, flies and other small arthropods is suitable and these should be dusted with a vitamin/mineral supplement. All species of *Anolis* lay small clutches of 1–3 eggs repeatedly during the breeding season, which extends throughout spring and summer. Incubation data is lacking: at present, *Anolis* species are so numerous that there is little incentive to breed them seriously.

Lizards of the genus *Sceloporus* are known as swifts or spiny lizards. A group of smaller species is also known collectively as fence lizards. These small to medium-sized lizards are covered in large pointed scales, giving a spiky appearance. Many occur in the drier parts of North America, especially around rock outcrops, but others are found in the more humid regions of Central America. Several, such as Yarrow's swift, *S. jarrovii*, are montane forms. Males are invariably more brightly coloured than their female counterparts and several are especially attractive, for instance, the granite spiny lizard, *S. orcutti*, in which males are metallic blue-green and *S. malachitus*, in which they are metallic emerald green. Even the more dingy-looking species may have patches of bright colour, often blue, on their throats and bellies, and these are displayed when the lizard advertises his ownership of a territory by bobbing up and down. The brightest colours, however, are

50. Western fence lizard, *Sceloporus occidentalis*.

only apparent when the lizards are healthy and not subject to stress. Like other iguanids, the males are highly territorial and only one should be kept in each cage. They fare well in a spacious vivarium furnished with a substrate of gravel and a jumble of rocks in which to hide. A background temperature of about 25°C should be maintained, with a hot-spot of at least 35°C in part of the cage. A drop in temperature at night will be beneficial and most, if not all, species benefit from slightly cooler conditions in the winter. They are all insectivorous.

In general, the montane forms give birth to live young and the lowland forms are oviparous. Although there is little data on captive reproduction, the live-bearing species appear to give birth to around six young whereas the egg-layers are rather more prolific, with clutches averaging about 12.

Staying in North America, there is a variety of small iguanids occupying desert and semi-desert habitats which occasionally find their way into the pet trade. Species such as the side-blotched lizard, *Uta stansburiana*, and the tree lizards and brush lizards, *Urosaurus*, differ only slightly in general appearance from the smaller species of

51.   The side-blotched lizard, *Uta stansburiana*, is a common small iguanid from North America.

52. One of several small iguanids from Chile, belonging to the genus *Liolaemus*, possibly *L. tenuis*.

Sceloporus and can be treated in exactly the same manner in captivity. These are all egg-laying lizards, and may lay several clutches throughout the spring and summer. They would appear to be ideal subjects for outdoor vivaria, open in the warmer parts of the world or glass-covered in more temperate regions.

In parts of South America, the members of the genus *Liolaemus* closely parallel the North American swifts, and are sometimes known as Chilean swifts (although they are also found in neighbouring countries). These species have only recently found their way into the pet trade, and many of the more attractive species are frequently available. Several of them are bright blue or green, often with other bright colours, such as orange, on their undersides. As usual, males are larger than females and far more colourful. Since the males and females differ so markedly it can sometimes be difficult to ensure that true pairs are obtained – females of the various species can look somewhat similar to each other, but very different to their male counterparts. This is especially problematical where dealers keep males and females of several species in the same cage. Indeed, species

130

53. A slightly larger Chilean swift, *Liolaemus* sp. Identification of these species can be difficult as collection data is rarely available.

identification can be difficult *per se* because of their great diversity and the wide variety of forms within each species: many which are frequently imported are undoubtedly wrongly named.

Both males and females are highly territorial and will not tolerate others of the same species and sex; a pecking order is quickly established and those at the bottom of it soon become stressed, emaciated and physically damaged. Although it may be possible to keep several pairs of different species in a large 'community' cage, this would need to be of an experimental nature, with the facility of separating them quickly should discord occur. They appear to require similar care to the *Sceloporus* species but, at present, little is known about the conditions necessary to induce them to breed. It is suggested that they be given a fairly cool background temperature, a hot-spot of at least 35°C during the day and an insectivorous diet. It may also be necessary to cool them down during the winter but, since they originate in the southern hemisphere, their biological rhythm may override any such manipulations. Like the *Sceloporus* species, there are live-bearing as well as egg-laying species in this genus and it is suspected that there is a correlation with altitude, those occurring at higher elevations being the ones most likely to give birth to live young. This is an interesting group of lizards about which little appears to be known. Considering the huge numbers which are currently in circulation, it would be a great pity if amateurs do not take the opportunity to contribute towards an understanding of their biology.

Yet another grouping of North American iguanids may be recognised: these are the medium-sized species with smooth granular scales, long hind legs and large heads. Gathered together under this description can be found genera such as *Crotaphytus*, the collared lizards, *Gambelia*, the leopard lizards, *Callisaurus*, the zebra-tailed lizard, *Uma*, the fringe-toed lizards, *Holbrookia* and *Cophosaurus*, the earless lizards and *Petrosaurus*, the rock lizards. Despite their diversity (and several are highly specialised), they have certain similarities which bear upon their care and maintenance. All grow in excess of 30 cm, although much of this measurement consists of tail, all are desert or semi-desert species requiring hot conditions and all are carnivorous, eating small rodents and lizards as well as insects. In addition, all are attractive and worth keeping and breeding, although a number are rare in the wild and trade in them is restricted.

These species all require very large cages due to their active lifestyles: if they are confined too closely they will become stressed. A cage measuring $100 \times 50 \times 50$ cm is an absolute minimum for one or two of any of these species. If possible, a cage measuring twice this size will enable them to behave more naturally and will increase the chances of their settling in well and possibly breeding. Apart from their water bowl, they should be kept under totally dry conditions and so the cage must be well-ventilated and should have a background temperature of at least 25°C during the day; a drop in temperature during the night will not cause any problems. In addition, a powerful spotlight, giving a hot-spot of at least 40°C is essential. Additional lighting, in the form of one or more tubes giving off plenty of ultra-violet radiation, is equally important.

The diet of these lizards should consist of large insects such as crickets and locusts, but can be supplemented with young rodents when available. Vitamin and mineral preparations should be added to their food regularly. On no account should they be kept in the same cage as other, smaller, species of lizards. Breeding takes place in the spring, and all species lay eggs. Unfortunately, none of them are widely bred in captivity at present, but it is logical to suppose that they would require a period of cooler conditions in the winter, accompanied by shorter days. Adequate feeding, plenty of calcium and plenty of ultra-violet are almost certainly the other important factors.

Although the above basic requirements are fairly constant across all the species listed, the way in which their vivaria are furnished varies

54. Zebra-tailed lizard, *Callisaurus draconoides*.

55. Earless lizard, *Holbrookia maculata*.

56.   Collared lizard, *Crotaphytus collaris*, an attractive species which requires a very large cage and high temperatures if it is to thrive.

from genus to genus according to the way in which they have adapted to the various habitats in which they are found. The most general-purpose species are *Crotaphytus*, *Gambelia*, *Cophosaurus* and *Holbrookia*. These are equally well catered for with a substrate of gravel, sand or a mixture of the two. Several large rocks should be placed in the cage, at least one of which should be positioned under the spotlight. A cave or crevice should also be created from the rocks and the lizards will retire into this once the light has gone out and the basking rock has cooled down. *Uma* and *Callisaurus* require a more open arrangement, with a substrate of sand. This sand should be of a free-running variety, as used for horticultural purposes, for instance silver sand, rather than builders' sand which has a tendency to form solid lumps after it has become wet. Zebra-tailed lizards will also require one or two rocks on which to perch, but the fringe-toed lizards are content with a good depth of sand and a single, large, flat rock. They have tiny scales forming a fringe along the edges of their toes; these enable them to run rapidly across fine, loose sand and their escape strategy is to dive into the sand in order to take cover. They will spend the night in a permanent burrow beneath the flat rock. *Petrosaurus thalassinus* is a

57. Round-tailed horned lizard, *Phrynosoma modestum* .

58. A newly born short-horned lizard, *Phrynosoma douglassii*, the only live-bearing horned lizard species.

large and impressive lizard from Baja California, often known as the Baja blue rock lizard. As its name suggests, it has several blue areas over its body, mainly around the head, neck and upper parts of the back. Males have more blue areas than females, although the females are also attractive. A second species, the banded rock lizard, *P. mearnsi*, is found further north and, although not so large or colourful, would also make an interesting exhibit. Both species are greatly flattened from top to bottom, an adaptation to living behind huge flakes of rock which have partially broken away from canyon walls due to erosion. In order to display these lizards effectively, the cage should be as tall as possible, and vertical clefts should be created by cementing thin slabs of stone on to the back wall, which should also be covered in stonework. The spotlight should be directed at a section of this artificial rockface so that the lizards can bask while clinging to the vertical surface. These species live in rather more humid surroundings than the others in this group. It would probably be beneficial to spray their cages from time to time.

The lizards belonging to the genus *Phrynosoma* are among the most unusual iguanids. Fourteen species are recognised, ranging from the northern parts of the United States down into Mexico. They are commonly known as horned lizards or horned 'toads' and have disc-shaped bodies, wide spiny heads and short tails. They are mostly desert species, all rely heavily on camouflage to escape the attentions of predators and they specialise in eating ants. Among their more remarkable characteristics is the ability to squirt blood from their eyes if they are tormented, although this has only been recorded in two or three species and captives hardly ever perform. In the past, all these species earned themselves a reputation for being impossible to maintain in captivity. In recent years, however, a better understanding of the requirements of desert lizards has resulted in limited success with these species. Most importantly, they require extremely hot daytime temperatures: a hot-spot of at least 40°C should be created, using a powerful spotlight. Background temperature is less important because they experience cold nights in the wild, and a small heat pad placed under one end of their cage will suffice. Ultra-violet light is essential and at least one blacklight should be installed 15–30 cm above the surface on which the lizards bask. A natural set-up is possible for these lizards and may well be essential. The cage should be covered with about 5 cm of sand, grit or lava; the lizards will bury themselves in this at night. In the morning they will push their heads through the surface and begin to warm up, eventually emerging completely, flatten their bodies and orientate them towards the heat source. A small pile of rocks will give them somewhere to forage and a basking surface. Succulent plants, especially cacti, can be left in their pots and plunged into the substrate or wedged in between the rocks but some means of preventing the lizards from burrowing into the compost must be found.

Although horned lizards eat mainly ants in nature, they will also accept other insects, including small crickets, waxworms, mealworms, etc. They have large stomachs and require huge quantities of food, typically gorging themselves on vast numbers of small prey items in a single sitting. Food should be dusted with a vitamin/mineral powder as for other iguanids.

There is little sexual dimorphism in these species but males can usually be distinguished by the presence of femoral and pre-anal pores. Breeding takes place in the spring and large clutches of eggs are laid about one month later. It is not known whether females lay more than one clutch each year. One species, the short-horned lizard, *Phrynosoma douglassii*, lives in a montane habitat and gives birth to about 20 live young, each with a body roughly the size of a human thumbnail. Rearing young horned lizards will certainly present problems if they are denied access to heat and ultra-violet. Regular breeding has not been achieved yet but would make a worthwhile, if time-consuming, project.

In summary, the small iguanids form a diverse and interesting group of lizards which would repay further study by herpetoculturalists. Unfortunately, they have, until recently at least, been regarded as easily expendable pet-trade items and little effort has been made to breed them in captivity. This is a great shame, and many species are now becoming almost impossible to obtain as they are justifiably protected in their natural habitats. A desire to keep them in captivity carries with it a responsibility to maintain them well and, especially, to make every effort to create the conditions necessary to induce them to breed.

CHAPTER 14

Agamids

The Agamidae is a family of about 300 species which are restricted to the Old World (Europe, Africa, Asia and Australasia). Many species closely parallel iguanids and the whole family is an Old World counterpart of them. Because they are so varied, there is no one obvious characteristic which sets them apart from other lizards, and they have no collective common name.

They vary in size from under 30 cm to over 1 metre and many species have crests and frills. Almost all are carnivorous, although some will also eat a small amount of vegetation and members of one genus are entirely herbivorous. Most lay eggs, but members of the genus, *Phrynocephalus*, and the species *Cophotis ceylanica*, which do not concern us here, give birth to live young.

One species, *Liolepis belliana*, may be able to reproduce parthenogenetically (see Chapters 16 and 17).

The species are divided into two sections: those which are herbivorous and those which are carnivorous.

1: THE LARGE HERBIVOROUS SPECIES

Despite the large number of species contained within the family Agamidae, the members of only one genus, *Uromastyx*, are entirely herbivorous. These impressive lizards, variously known as mastigures or dab lizards, are found throughout the belt of arid desert and steppe which covers much of North Africa, the Middle East and northern parts of the Indian sub-continent. They are totally diurnal in their activity patterns, retreating into burrows at night or during cooler weather, where they are buffered from extremes of cold. During the day they bask in the most intense heat, with body temperatures exceeding 40°C at times. In this respect they closely parallel several of the North American and Australian lizards. The genus is divided into about ten species although the classification is rather uncertain in one or two cases. Only a small number of these are ever available through the pet trade and then only occasionally.

In captivity, their main requirements are bright light, plenty of heat and a roomy cage. Mercury vapour lamps are probably the best way of producing the intensity of lighting essential to normal activity, while an ultra-violet fluorescent tube, or possibly a bank of several tubes, is equally important in order to allow the lizards to synthesise vitamin D3. In addition, background heating in the form of underfloor heat pads should be installed to maintain a background temperature of 25–30°C. There should be at least one hot-spot of 45°C minimum and all heating and lighting equipment should be placed at the same end of the cage so that the lizards will be able to bask in heat and light simultaneously, or retreat to a cooler, shadier area if desired. An artificial burrow should be available so that the lizards can retreat naturally at night; this can consist, most simply, of a wooden box with an opening in one side or, more elaborately, a compartment constructed beneath or to one side of the main cage and entered via an earthenware tube such as a section of drainpipe. Although at least some species hibernate in the wild, it is recommended that high daytime temperatures be maintained throughout the year and that, if it is hoped to induce breeding behaviour, only the light cycle is manipulated, reducing this to eight hours of light in winter and increasing it gradually to 16 hours of light at the height of summer.

Naturalistic cage embellishments should be kept to a minimum. A few heavy rocks on a substrate of coarse gravel or newspaper are really all that is practicable; living plants will be eaten, if they do not wither and die first.

Although juvenile mastigures (and adults of the smaller species) will sometimes accept a limited amount of insect food, such as crickets, locusts and waxworms, the main bulk of food will consist of vegetation. This should be as varied as possible to ensure a balanced diet. Leguminous plants such as clover and the seed pods of peas and beans are probably fairly close to their natural diet, but they will take almost any plant material as long as it is not distasteful or poisonous. The food should not be limited to fresh, green vegetation but should include coarser material such as hay, dried cereal and flowers. As with many herbivorous species, yellow flowers, especially dandelion, are relished. All meals should be fortified with a mineral powder containing plenty of calcium and additional vitamins should also be added regularly, especially if the lizards' access to ultra-violet is limited. Wild mastigures appear to obtain almost all of their water requirement from their diet or from drinking droplets of dew which form on their scales (and there is evidence that the scales are arranged in such a way that a matrix of channels directs water into the corners of their mouths through capillary action). In captivity, they rarely drink from a water bowl although they will often sit in the water and appear to soak themselves. An occasional spraying with warm water would appear to be useful and this should be directed straight on to the lizards.

Unfortunately, the conditions required to induce these lizards to breed are poorly understood. Although one or two zoos have managed to obtain small numbers of offspring, institutes which are situated within their natural range (and can therefore keep them under semi-natural conditions outside) are the only ones to have had any degree of regular breeding successes. Indeed, reliable methods of sexing have yet to be established; adults which develop larger heads and more powerful necks are assumed to be males but, due to the lack of breeding success, this can rarely be confirmed.

Representative species

Only three species are commonly seen in captivity, and these are only available spasmodically. Due to their poor captive-breeding record, the trade in these species relies on wild-caught specimens. *Uromastyx hardwickii* is a common lizard in the sandy parts of northwestern India and Pakistan. It is the smallest species, growing to a total length of around 30 cm, and is yellowish brown in colour. The young are said to have dark spots along the back. *U. aegypticus* is much larger, growing approximately twice as long as Hardwick's dab lizard and is proportionately more heavily built. It, too, is a fairly uniform light brown in colour although the juveniles have faint mottled markings.

Uromastyx acanthinurus is the most spectacular of the three available species. It can exceed 60 cm in total length and occurs in a variety of colour forms. Although the ground colour is brown, when warm the lizards are suffused with red, orange, yellow or lime green. There appears to be no correlation with the sexes, and the colour differences may reflect geographical variation, although this is not clear at present.

2: CARNIVOROUS AGAMIDS

The *Uromastyx* species dealt with above are somewhat atypical: the vast majority of the 300 or so species of agamids are carnivorous and among them are several species which are well-suited to vivarium

59. Juvenile Egyptian mastigure, *Uromastyx aegypticus*.

culture. A large number of species hail from Australia and the exportation of these species has been severely restricted for a number of years. This has led to a great deal of interest in breeding these species, some of which are now widely available in Europe and North America as a result of captive-breeding. This situation is an encouraging sign that lizards can be successfully bred in captivity on a fairly large scale, provided there is sufficient incentive to do so. It also contrasts most markedly with the situation regarding Asian agamids (and other reptiles) which are still collected on a huge scale and distributed throughout the world's pet trade on a 'disposable commodity' basis. In keeping with this situation, there is far more hard information available relating to the care and breeding of some of these Australian species than to Asian and African species.

It is not possible to give generalised instructions for the maintenance of the carnivorous agamids: the species are too diverse with respect to their size and to their needs. The requirements of a number of the more commonly kept and bred species will therefore be dealt with in some detail in the hope that this information can be used to cover the similar species which may occur occasionally.

60. *Uromastyx acanthinurus*, a herbivorous agamid.

Representative species

Amongst the larger agamids, the Australian bearded dragons, genus *Pogona*, are probably the most popular. They adapt well to captivity, provided a few simple rules are obeyed, become tame easily and breed readily. Although there is some confusion over the taxonomy of these species, it seems likely that the species most commonly seen is *P. vitticeps*; other bearded dragons are rather similar in size and appearance and their requirements can be assumed to be broadly similar.

Adult bearded dragons are large and impressive lizards. They grow to a total length of approximately 50 cm, of which about half is tail. They are heavily built, with a broad head, stocky body and thick tail. A row of small spines runs around the rim of the back and other groups of spines are found at the back of the head and around the jowls. Their most famous characteristic, however, is the 'beard', a fold of skin on the throat which is covered with small pointed scales. When the throat is puffed out, the scales stand on end and the lizard looks as though it is wearing a spiky beard. The throat is usually dark, often black, but the colour and markings on the back are variable, hence the problems

61. Various species of bearded dragons, such as *Pogona vitticeps*, are bred successfully in captivity.

associated with species identification. The normal coloration of *P. vitticeps* is pale brown or buff with a darker vertebral stripe. On either side of the stripe there are lighter markings which may take the form of crossbars. Some individuals are suffused with yellow or orange, these colours being especially intense when the animals display. Juveniles are pale brown with darker markings, and lack the beard.

Pogona vitticeps and other closely related bearded dragons inhabit the semi-desert regions of Central Australia, and often take up basking and display positions on tree stumps, prominent rocks or fence posts. Males are territorial and display by inflating their throat and bobbing their head. Subordinate males are sometimes tolerated outside the breeding season but fights often ensue and they are best kept separately in captivity. Females are also territorial but it is usually permissible to keep several of them together with a single male because once a pecking order is established subordinate females are not harassed to any great extent.

This species is not particularly active and requires less room than some other lizards of a similar size. They should, however, be given ample

143

space to behave naturally and a breeding pair or trio should not be kept in a cage measuring less than 150 × 60 cm. They require a substrate of gravel or sand, or an artificial alternative such as corn cob granules or compressed sawdust pellets may be used. One or two large rocks or pieces of dead wood will enhance the appearance of the set-up and provide the lizards with opportunities to climb. A powerful heat-lamp or spotlight should be placed directly above one of these perches and a hot-spot of 40–50°C should be created during the day. A powerful ultra-violet lamp, such as a blacklight, should be turned on at the same time as the heat-lamp, and should be installed above the basking positions. Background temperature during the summer should be 25°C in the coolest part of the cage, but should be allowed to drop to about 20°C for a month or two during the winter if they are to breed successfully.

These lizards will eat almost anything. They relish large insects such as crickets, locusts and mealworms but will also accept canned pet food and pieces of meat. In addition, vegetable material such as chopped fruit, vegetables and flowers should be given to provide a balanced diet. All meals should be fortified with a vitamin and mineral supplement, vitamin D3 and calcium being most important.

Breeding behaviour commences as soon as the temperature is raised during late winter/early spring, and continues throughout the summer, with each female laying several clutches. As egg-laying approaches the females become noticeably swollen in the lower abdomen and begin to search for a suitable egg-laying site. A large container of moist sand should be placed in the cage at this time and this will normally be used in preference to the dry substrate in the cage. The eggs are laid in a chamber and covered over after laying; clutches from large females can exceed 30 eggs, although an average of about 20 is more usual. These should be removed from the egg-laying container and incubated in moist vermiculite, as described in Chapter 7. At a temperature of 32°C they hatch in about 60 days.

The hatchlings measure about 10 cm in total length and their markings are more distinct than those of the adults. They can be reared in small groups in open cages with a substrate of sand and pieces of wood for basking and for hiding beneath. Ultra-violet light is essential and a blacklight, or similar equipment should be suspended a few centimetres above their basking site. Background heating, provided by underfloor heat pads for instance, should be maintained at 25–30°C, while a hot-spot of 40–45°C should be created with a spotlight or heat-lamp. Young bearded dragons are more insectivorous than the adults and will usually only accept crickets, waxworms,

62.   Newly hatched *Pogona vitticeps* are more distinctively marked than adults but lack the beard.

mealworms and so on at first. As they grow they can be offered greens and fruit and, eventually, weaned on to canned food if required. A strict regime of dusting the food with vitamins and minerals is essential at this time if they are to grow without deformities; extra calcium can be added to the diet by means of grated cuttlefish bone.

Some individuals feed and grow better than others and these will become dominant in the groups. Small and subordinate youngsters

145

must be removed if they appear to be stressed (reluctant to feed and bask) and every effort should be made to ensure that each individual is obtaining plenty of food, vitamins and minerals. The young are tame almost as soon as they hatch and quickly learn to take food from the fingers so there is no excuse for allowing the weaker individuals to get left behind by their clutch-mates. If fed adequately, the young grow very quickly and will need to be moved on to progressively larger cages. Under normal circumstances, numbers will gradually reduce as surplus animals are disposed of to other collectors. They can reach sexual maturity in about one year, at which time the males may be distinguishable by their larger heads, darker throats and behaviour patterns.

As far as is known, other species of bearded dragons will breed in captivity under exactly the same conditions as *Pogone vitticeps*. The archetypal bearded dragon is *P. barbatus*, formerly known as *Amphibolurus barbatus* and this species grows to about the same size as *P. vitticeps*. Other species are slightly smaller and may be difficult to identify.

One other Australian agamid should be mentioned here, although it is rarely seen in captivity. This is *Chlamydosaurus kingii*, the frilled lizard. This large and spectacular species thrives under similar conditions to the bearded dragons and captive breeding has been achieved on a few occasions. It seems likely that, once breeding and rearing methods have been refined, it too will slowly work its way into the pet trade, albeit in small numbers. This species requires more space than the *Pogona* species because it is larger and more active. Captive-bred individuals become tame, and rarely erect the large ruff around their throat which gives them their common name.

Of the remaining larger species of agamids, the water dragons, *Physignathus*, are the ones most likely to be seen in captivity. In particular, the Thai species, *P. cocincinus*, is still imported in fair numbers and is also bred in captivity. This species is superficially similar to the South American iguanas and basilisks and grows to a total length of 50 cm, of which more than half is tail. The hind legs are greatly elongated and are almost as long as the head and body. It is predominantly green and has a dorsal crest consisting of a single row of enlarged spines. There is a slight hump on the neck and the spines here are enlarged. The chin is white and the throat is white or pale yellow. Males are larger and have a more pronounced dorsal crest. Juveniles have diagonal bands across their flanks which disappear with age.

Imported adult animals are likely to be in poor shape, often with

63. Asian, or Thai, water dragon, *Physignathus cocincinus*.

damaged snouts due to constant chaffing on collecting bags and poor cages, and usually with their fair share of internal parasites. Juveniles, either wild-caught or, preferably, captive-bred, are therefore the best buy. As their name implies, these species are semi-aquatic and require a large pool of water in their cage. The cage itself should also be large, at least 1.5 metres long and, since they are arboreal in their habitats, it should be at least one metre high for one or two adults. It should be furnished with branches to the top where the lizards can bask under a heat-lamp or spotlight during the day. A background temperature of 25–30°C is needed at all times. Normal lighting should be supplemented with a blacklight or another good source of ultra-violet. The bottom of the cage may be covered with coarse gravel, bark chippings or newspaper.

Water dragons are mainly carnivorous but will accept a certain amount of vegetable material. A good diet for juveniles consists of crickets, locusts and waxworms, heavily dusted with a vitamin and mineral supplement. As they grow they will gradually begin to accept some soft fruit and some will also take young rodents and even canned pet food. Fish can also be offered and many will accept this, but it

147

should not be used exclusively as this will lead to nutritional deficiencies.

Breeding takes place during the cooler months, i.e. winter and early spring. In the course of a single breeding season, each female can lay up to 5 clutches of about 10–15 eggs, which are buried in damp sand. A suitable egg-laying container should be placed in a secluded part of the cage when she begins to swell with eggs. The eggs should be removed as soon as they are found, and incubated at a temperature of 28–30°C. They hatch after about 60 days, but several breeders have found that a proportion of the eggs invariably develop to full term and then fail to hatch. The cause of this is uncertain but may be associated with the large numbers of eggs laid over a fairly short period of time, coupled with inadequate feeding of the female, especially with regard to vitamin D3 and calcium: more research needs to be carried out in order to correct this problem.

The hatchings measure approximately 15 cm in total length but are spindly, giving the impression that the hind legs are excessively long. They should be reared in small groups, fed on insects dusted with a vitamin/calcium supplement and given access to ultra-violet. If they can be persuaded to accept newborn mice as soon as they are large enough their growth rate will improve and the chances of nutritional problems and deformities will be minimised. Sexual maturity can be attained in just over one year, by which time the youngsters should have grown to about 40 cm in total length.

A second species of *Physignathus* occurs in Australia. This is the eastern water dragon, *P. lesueurii*, which is of a similar size but brown in colour. Its back and tail are marked with broad black and narrow white crossbars and there may be a black bar connecting the eye to the side of the neck. The throat and underside may be green, orange or blood red. A dorsal crest of enlarged tooth-like scales runs from the nape of the neck down on to the tail, as in the Asian species. Although rarely seen outside Australia, this species requires similar conditions to *P. cocincinus*, although one would expect it be to rather more tolerant with regard to temperature.

A wide variety of the smaller Asian agamids are likely to occur occasionally in the pet trade. Their maintenance depends to some extent on their habitat and this can be difficult to establish since their natural history is so little known. Many specimens are also incorrectly identified. Members of genera such as *Calotes* are arboreal and should be given high cages with plenty of perches. Their basic requirements are similar to those of the water dragons, except that they do not require a large pool of water but should be liberally sprayed instead.

64. Eastern water dragon, *Physignathus lesueurii*, from Australia.

65. The mountain horned lizard, *Acanthosaura crucigera*, from Southeast Asia, is an interesting species which appears to require rather specialised attention: breeding in captivity has probably not been achieved yet.

66. The sail-fin lizard, *Hydrosaurus pustulosus*, is a large and spectacular agamid from Asian rainforests. Although it is a rare species, captive-bred juveniles, such as this one, are sometimes available due to the breeding successes of several zoos and private collectors in Europe. It should be treated in the same way as the water dragons but requires a very large cage.

151

67. Starred agama, *Agama stellio*, the only member of this large family which strays into Europe.

They are insectivorous but some may also eat small rodents and possibly soft fruit.

Terrestrial agamids include members of the nominate genus *Agama*. These are typically about 30 cm in total length and have heterogeneous scales: that is, the scales are of different sizes and shapes, with some being tuberculate, others spiny. Their tails are often heavily armoured, with rings of spines. Their legs are long and powerful for fast running and their digits and claws are also long, for climbing. Some are semi-arboreal and others climb over rock outcrops but, in general, they come from desert or semi-desert environments and should be kept more or less dry. Males of all these species are more brightly coloured than females and have characteristic displays in which the head and forepart of the body is raised off the ground repeatedly in the form of push-ups. The North African species, such as the rainbow lizard, *Agama agama*, tend to be more brightly coloured but more demanding in their requirements than those from southeastern Europe and the Middle East.

All species are active and require very large cages with a substrate of sand or gravel. Only one male must be kept in each cage and females may also be subject to harassment and stress if more than one is present. Single pairs are therefore the best arrangement. Rocks, large pieces of bogwood or branches should be placed in the cage for basking and display, and a powerful heat-lamp should be directed towards at least one of these to provide a hot-spot of 35–40°C. Their dietary requirements are straightforward as they will eat crickets and waxworms readily, and some will also accept plant material in the forms of leaves and flowers of plants such as dandelion. Vitamin and mineral supplements are essential if they are to thrive and breed, as is a powerful blacklight. In warmer climates, several of these species could probably be kept in outdoor enclosures, especially if they were protected from extremes of cold by means of removable glass frames.

Breeding takes place in the spring and summer and females may lay two or three clutches each year. There are normally 10 or more eggs in each clutch and these are buried in damp sand, which must be provided for this purpose. They are removed for incubation in damp vermiculite and hatch after about 50 days at a temperature of 28–30°C. The young may be reared together for a short time but quickly develop a dominance hierarchy, with subordinate animals becoming stressed and emaciated. If this occurs they should be split up into groups of two or three lizards of similar size, or moved to a very large enclosure where each can find a territory. Sexual maturity is reached in one year if they are well fed.

Since captive-bred agamas are rarely available, all newly acquired individuals should be assumed to be carrying internal parasites, mostly nematode worms and flagellates. Regular dosing with the appropriate medication, as outlined in Chapter 8, is therefore necessary if these are to be eliminated.

CHAPTER 15

Skinks

The large family Scincidae contains about 1,000 members scattered across the world. Despite their number, most are easily recognisable as skinks due to certain characteristics which are fairly constant throughout the family. These include smooth shiny scales, a cylindrical body, short legs (sometimes the complete absence of legs) and sombre coloration. Many of them are small in size, often with long tails, and the majority of species are secretive inhabitants of leaf-litter and dense vegetation. They may also be found beneath logs and stones, under bark or below the surface in sandy regions. Some are adept 'sand-swimmers' spending their entire lives in dunes of loose windblown sand, through which they travel rapidly by wriggling their body.

Skinks make good vivarium subjects, having important advantages over several other groups of lizards. Although some of the larger and more spectacular species have always been popular with lizard-keepers, the smaller species have been largely neglected. Many of these, however, are also worth keeping as, although they may not all be brightly coloured, they adapt well to captivity, can be kept in colonies where interesting interactions can be observed, and often breed readily. They have the distinct advantage of requiring less ultra-violet than most other lizards, and some can probably function normally without it altogether. The diet of most is easily obtainable.

Several species from Australia are distinct with regard to size and also their captive requirements. This group will be dealt with first, before moving on to the other, mostly smaller, species.

1: LARGE AUSTRALASIAN SKINKS

These skinks occupy a special place in the reptile hobby. They are amongst the most impressive and most easily kept species, are interesting and attractive and become quite tame. Because they are not freely available, they are expensive and should be given the very best care and attention, with the ultimate aim of breeding from them.

The large species belonging to the genus *Tiliqua* are commonly known as blue-tongue skinks; all except one of them come from Australia (*T. gigas* is from New Guinea). *T. gerrardii* is a slightly smaller, more slender species from Australia, known as the pink-tongued skink, and the stump-tailed skink, *Tiliqua rugosus* (also known as *Trachydosaurus rugosus*), is also Australian. *Tiliqua* also contains a few smaller skinks which are not included here.

The blue-tongued skinks are large, heavy-bodied species growing to a maximum length of 40–45 cm, of which about one-third consists of tail. Their heads are large and spade-shaped, those of the males often being more massive compared to those of the females. The body is roughly cylindrical, but slightly compressed from top to bottom, and the limbs are relatively short. They move with a ponderous gait but are capable of rapid lunges. Coloration depends on the species and the following is only a brief account which may serve to identify them.

The eastern blue-tongued skink, *Tiliqua scincoides*, is a grey or pale brown above with seven to ten prominent dark crossbars on the back, these becoming oblique on the flanks. A dark band runs from the snout, through the eye and on to the temporal region. The western blue-tongued skink, *T. occipitalis*, is tan or pale brown with four to six

68.   The blotched blue-tongued skink, *Tiliqua nigrolutea*, is one of the most attractive and desirable of the large Australian skinks.

69. New Guinea blue-tongued skink, *Tiliqua gigas*.

broad dark bands across the body and a further three to five dark bands encircling the tail. A wide dark line runs through the eye, as in the previous species. The central blue-tonged skink, *T. multifasciata*, is pale grey or brown above with about seven broad bands of pale orange or tan running across the body and a further series of bands of the same colour on the tail. The body bands are broad on the dorsal surface but become more narrow on the flanks. The head is marked with a dark wedge-shaped band running through the eye. The blotched blue-tongued skink, *T. nigrolutea*, is dark brown or black with several pairs of large cream or pale pink blotches running down the back. These may develop into streaks towards the tail. The flanks have irregular pale mottled markings, and the throat is white. There is no temporal band through the eye. The New Guinea species, *T. gigas*, is grey or grey-brown with irregular narrow bands of dark brown across the back. These markings become obscure in some adults.

The pink-tongued skink, *Tiliqua gerrardii*, has a smaller body but a longer tail: its total length is therefore similar to the other species, about 40 cm, but its weight is far less. This species is variable but is usually grey or brown above with a number of wide dark bars running across the back and obliquely backwards on the flanks. It lacks the

70. The unmistakable stump-tailed skink, *Tiliqua rugosus*.

temporal streak through the eye. Whereas the other large species are totally terrestrial, this one is semi-arboreal in habits, hence the longer tail, which is prehensile, and the more slender body. It is largely nocturnal, in contrast to the other species, which are strictly diurnal.

The stump-tailed skink, *Tiliqua rugosus*, is totally different in appearance to any of the blue-tongues (and, indeed, to any other lizard). The characteristic which sets it apart, and makes it instantly recognisable, is its covering of large, rough scales. These give it its local name of shingle-back lizard, and the oft-repeated comparison to a pine cone. Its tail is short, blunt and flattened; this acts as a storage organ and becomes heavily swollen when the animal is in good condition. In colour it may be totally jet black, black or brown with a scattering of bone-coloured scales, or predominantly off-white with small dark brown blotches. It is slow-moving and diurnal.

Care and breeding of these lizards is basically similar. Because they are not especially active, large cages are unnecessary: a cage measuring about 1 × 1.5 metres is adequate for a pair or small group of adults, and height is not important as, except in the case of the pink-tongued skink, they never climb. The latter species appreciates some branches to clamber over and the cage should be tall enough to accommodate these. Cage substrate can consist of coarse gravel, horticultural clay beads or bark chippings. Furnishings should be kept to a minimum for ease of cleaning and these are most simply provided by half-round clay drain-pipes, under which the lizards can retreat. Similar lengths of cork bark can also be used to serve this purpose but will be moved around by the activity of the skinks, are more difficult to clean efficiently and should be replaced occasionally. Background temperatures need not be high, about 20°C being adequate, and this should be created by heat pads placed under (or in) one part of the cage, thereby allowing the skinks to raise their body temperatures by moving over or on to them. Lighting should be provided by a natural spectrum fluorescent tube, without which young animals may become deformed and adults will not breed successfully.

With the exception of *Tiliqua gerrardii*, these skinks are omnivorous in their diet and will eat insects, small rodents, minced meat, canned pet food, fruit and vegetables. There is often a temptation to feed them a high protein diet in order to accelerate growth rates, but this leads to obesity and is unnatural anyway. A good basic diet consists of about 25 per cent minced meat or chopped rodents, 25 per cent soft fruit and 50 per cent coarse vegetation such as beans and peas (and their pods), root vegetables, leaves and stalks. They will also accept pelleted fish and reptile food but these are too high in protein to be fed other than as an occasional treat, which will help to tame them. Insects are also welcomed but are expensive given the large appetites of the lizards. They should be fed two or three times each week; more frequently for juveniles which are growing and for pregnant females. Most of these species come from arid environments and drink very little, but water should be offered, either in a bowl or, occasionally, as a thorough spraying of the cage.

The pink-tongued skink, *T. gerrardii*, is, by nature, a dietary specialist, feeding almost exclusively on land molluscs. Some individuals will refuse to take anything other than live slugs and snails and this can be a problem during the colder months when these items are hard to find. Most, however, will take frozen slugs and snails (a stock should be built up when they are plentiful), while others will reluctantly accept substitutes in the form of shellfish (mussels, cockles and so on) and newborn mice and rats. All species should be given dietary supplements such as a multivitamin powder with added calcium once each week.

Their natural breeding season is spring and summer, bearing in mind that the seasons are reversed in Australia. Wild-caught animals moved to the northern hemisphere may shift their breeding season slightly in keeping with the natural light/temperature cycles here, mating from December through until the early spring. Captive-bred animals, however, can be treated as though they were native, i.e. they mate in the northern spring and early summer. In order to induce breeding activity it is necessary to reduce the temperature during the winter. *T. nigrolutea* is very cold-tolerant: it should be cooled to 10–13°C for three months. The other species are probably not so hardy and their temperature should be reduced only slightly, to 13–18°C for the same period of time. Mating takes place within one month of warming the lizards up in the spring.

Sexing is by no means easy. As keepers become familiar with their animals they can often distinguish a subtle difference in the body shape of the males and females, with females being more portly whereas males have more or less parallel flanks. Head size seems to be an unreliable method of sexing, except in the case of the stump-tailed skink in which old males have greatly swollen jowls. Sexing can be carried out by means of an endoscope, or by monitoring hormone levels, but these techniques are beyond the scope of most collectors. With practice, the hemipenes of young animals can be everted by applying pressure at the base of the tail but, again, this technique is an acquired art and by no means simple. If animals are obtained from an experienced breeder, he or she should be able to make a fairly educated guess as to their sexes but the only sure way of knowing is to wait until the first breeding season, observe the behaviour of the various individuals and, ultimately, see which ones give birth!

Males are territorial and become aggressive during the breeding season. Although they can be kept in groups at other times, fighting may break out occasionally, especially when new individuals are added to the group. Some breeders keep their animals individually, putting males and females together for short periods during the breeding season. Under these conditions, matings often take place immediately and the animals can be separated again afterwards. Multiple matings are advised as fertility appears to be low and females which have only mated once or twice will rarely give birth. If the animals are kept together permanently as a breeding group, this problem is unlikely to arise, but care must be taken to ensure that excessive aggression does not lead to damage or stress in either the females or in subordinate males which may be present. Where aggression becomes severe, the animals may need to be separated and housed individually as described above, and this situation often develops in *Tiliqua scincoides* , one of the more highly territorial species.

During mating, the male grips the female around the neck in order to restrain her so that copulation can take place. This often results in superficial damage such as lost scales and old breeding animals often show scars from previous bouts. Where they are kept as a permanent group, missing scales on the neck and shoulder region are probably the best indication that mating has taken place.

All these skinks are live-bearing, with litter sizes depending on species. *Tiliqua rugosus* is the least productive with litters of only one or two enormous babies; *T. gigas, multifasciata, scincoides, intermedia* and *nigrolutea* typically have litters of 5–12, with larger females having the largest number of young, while *T. gerrardii* has large litters, averaging 15–25, but exceptionally 50 or more. Gestation periods are variable and probably depend on temperature. There is also a strong possibility that females are able to store sperm and so the period of time from mating to parturition need not necessarily represent the true gestation. As an indication, however, the average gestation period is around 100 days, but about 50 per cent longer in *T. gigas* and *T. rugosus*. Newborn young are approximately 16 cm long in the case of the blue-tongued skink, smaller, at about 10 cm in the pink-tongued skink (in keeping with the larger litter size) and about 18 cm in the stump-tailed skink.

The newborn young usually start to feed straight away, beginning with the membrane in which they are born. They grow more quickly if reared separately because their feeding habits can be more closely monitored – greedy individuals are less likely to monopolise the food supply. This system also avoids any possibility of fighting and associated stress. They grow steadily if fed on the diet outlined above, and will mature at eighteen months of age. Females can therefore give birth when they are two years old.

The Solomon Island skink, *Corucia zebrata*, is a strange and unique skink, endemic to the Solomon Islands. It is nocturnal and almost totally arboreal, and is sometimes known as the prehensile-tailed skink or the monkey-tailed skink. It can grow to 75 cm in total length but captives are usually rather smaller. The head is massive and wedge-shaped, the body cylindrical and the tail long and prehensile. Its limbs are long, for a skink, with well-developed claws on each digit. In colour it is greyish-green with indistinct mottled markings over the back of its body.

In captivity these skinks require a tall cage with an abundance of branches and vines in which to climb. Living plants with tough leaves, such as those belonging to the genera *Ficus* and *Philodenron* may be used to advantage, both to enhance the appearance of the cage and to provide cover for the lizards. The substrate of the cage can be of gravel, or an artificial material such as newspaper or compressed sawdust pellets. The background temperature should be maintained at about 25–30°C and a spotlight should be directed at one part of the cage so that the animals can bask and raise their body temperatures if they so wish. A blacklight is also recommended. They should be sprayed with water daily and will take most of their water requirement from the droplets which collect on the side of the cage, the branches or their own scales. This species is almost exclusively herbivorous and should be fed a mixture of root and leafy vegetables and soft fruit. Some will also accept eggs and others can be persuaded to take the occasional insect or newborn rodent. Vitamins and minerals, especially calcium, should be added to their diets.

Sexing this species can be difficult. Although males generally grow larger and have more powerful necks and jaws than the females, young males are virtually indistinguishable. They are, however, very territorial and two males will fight vigorously until one is removed. They may also show aggression to their keeper although there is much individual variation in this respect and some become very tame. Although they occasionally breed in captivity, this seems to occur more often by accident then by design. A single live young is born, measuring about one-third the length of the adults. Juveniles should be housed separately, but are otherwise treated in the same way as the adults.

All the species of skinks listed above are thought to be fairly closely related to one another, and to a fourth genus, *Egernia*. The 27 species of this genus are also Australasian, with all but one species occurring in Australia itself. There is some variation within the genus and several members do not look at all skink-like but closely parallel species in other diverse families from other parts of the world. Only a few species have reached the reptile hobby. The most frequently seen is Cunningham's skink, *E. cunninghami*. This species reaches a length of about 30 cm and its scales are heavily keeled and end in a sharp point. Those on the tail are especially spiky and the lizard bears a superficial resemblance to some of the larger *Sceloporus* species from North America (see Chapter 13). The coloration of this species is highly variable, ranging from a fairly uniform, mottled brown or grey, to a striking pattern of black and cream. Any markings which are present may be randomly distributed or they may consist of distinct stripes or crossbars. This and related species are rock-dwellers, living around outcrops and retreating into deep cracks and fissures when alarmed. Their spiny scales serve to wedge them tightly into place, while the tail may be curled around and used as a barricade.

Cages for *E. cunninghami* should be large and contain a jumble of

71.   The large and spectacular arboreal skink, *Corucia zebrata*, from the Solomon Islands, sometimes known as the monkey-tailed skink.

large rocks so that the lizards can behave naturally. Males are highly aggressive and only one can be kept in each cage; they can be recognised by their much broader heads and the development of heavy jowls as they mature. This is an omnivorous species and can be fed on a diet which is based on that recommended for blue-tongued skinks, including the addition of vitamin and mineral supplements, but more insects can be used since this species is a more active forager. Similarly, their requirements regarding temperature, lighting and a seasonal regime can be regarded as the same. Breeding takes place in the spring and early summer and litters of 4–6 live young are born after a gestation period of two to three months.

Egernia depressa is a much smaller species, growing to a total length of about 13 cm. It has a short, flattened tail, covered with long spiny scales. The scales on the back are also spiny, with a central keel and two smaller keels at either side. The scales are arranged in such a way that these keels form longitudinal ridges down the back and on to the tail. The markings consist of a pale brown to bright orange dorsal surface with narrow crossbands consisting of irregularly placed darker scales.

This species is similar to *E. cunninghami* in its habitat preference but is perhaps even more specialised. It rarely ventures more than a few inches from its retreat, in the wild or in captivity, and jams itself into a crevice at the slightest provocation. It needs hot dry conditions with an opportunity to bask in a hot-spot. It is almost entirely insectivorous and usually thrives in captivity, but they are hardly ever available and breeding successes have consequently been few and far between. Small litters of 1–3 live young are born after an indeterminate gestation period.

2: SMALLER SKINKS

The group of skinks dealt with above is a fairly small one, even though it includes the species likely to be of most interest to lizard-keepers. Of the remaining species, almost any can be kept successfully without too much trouble and many make interesting subjects. Their care and breeding will depend to a large extent on their origins: whether they are tropical or temperate; whether they are from an arid or humid environment; and whether they are arboreal, terrestrial or fossorial (burrowing).

The most straightforward species to keep are those from temperate grasslands, foothills and forests. North American species such as those belonging to the genus *Eumeces*, the southern African *Mabuya* species and the European *Chalcides* species can easily be accommodated in quite small vivaria of the basic fish-tank type. Many of them are unable to climb effectively so there may be no need for a lid, unless active insect food is to be used. The floor of the cage can be covered in fine gravel and this should have a layer of dead leaves or bracken over at least part of it. Pieces of bark or flat rocks should be scattered about to provide retreats, and living plants such as ivies and other tough species can be used, preferably plunged into the gravel complete with their pots. If a heat pad is placed under one half of the cage the lizards will be able to choose their optimum body temperature, while a spotlight should be installed and switched on during the day to allow them to bask; many will not bask in the open but prefer to move underneath a piece of bark or stone which has been warmed by the spotlight. A natural spectrum fluorescent tube will provide them with enough ultra-violet – powerful tubes such as the blacklights are probably unnecessary.

All these small species are insectivorous, and should be fed on crickets, locusts, waxworms and sweepings. These can be dusted with a vitamin/mineral preparation occasionally, although only breeding females seem to require large quantities of these supplements, especially calcium. Water should be present at all times and many of these species require rather humid conditions, so the cage should be thoroughly sprayed at regular intervals. Where possible, pieces of bark or stone should be lifted and the substrate beneath them sprayed so that these areas will remain permanently damp. This is particularly important where gravid females are present as they will require a moist substrate in which to deposit their eggs.

These species may be oviparous or viviparous. Even species within the same genus, e.g. *Mabuya*, may show both types of reproduction. Breeding takes place during the spring and it may be possible to distinguish males at this time of year due to their brighter coloration. For instance, in the North American broad-headed skink, *Eumeces laticeps* , the jowls of the male become flushed with orange at this time of year, and other instances of sexual dimorphism occur in other species. Where the males and females are similar in appearance it may be necessary to obtain a small group of animals and keep them together, observing their behaviour and removing any which are obviously being harassed: these will usually be subordinate males. Mating takes place in the spring, stimulated by warmer conditions and a longer daylength. Often this seasonal rhythm is retained even when the skinks are kept under fairly constant conditions all year round, but a deliberate cooling off period in the winter, accompanied by reducing the number of hours during which the spotlight is used will ensure synchronisation of breeding behaviour.

Certain of the North American *Eumeces* species lay their eggs in a small chamber under a piece of bark or stone and curl around them throughout the incubation period. There appears to have been no attempt to breed these species in captivity, which is a great shame since this degree of parental care is almost unique amongst lizards. Other species merely lay their eggs in a damp place and abandon them or, in the case of the live-bearing species, give birth in a secluded part of the cage. Unless there is a desire to allow those females which guard their eggs to do so naturally, any eggs should be removed for incubation as described in Chapter 7. There is practically no data available on incubation periods, but a temperature of 28–30°C is suggested as a starting-point.

Young of live-bearing species should be removed from their parents' cage and reared elsewhere. They should be cared for in the same way as the adults, but food should obviously be graded to an appropriate size. Vitamin and mineral supplements, and access to a source of ultra-violet is important if they are to be reared without deformities.

Tropical skinks, such as the *Mabuya* species from Southeast Asia and the *Riopa* species from tropical Africa, require rather more warmth and humidity. They should not, therefore, be kept in an open cage, although ventilation should be good. As before, a heat pad should be placed under part of the cage to allow the skinks to thermoregulate and a spotlight should be available for basking during the day. There should not be a substantial drop in temperature during the winter, however, although slightly cooler conditions may be helpful in stimulating breeding activity. Lighting should be good, and is best provided by a natural spectrum tube. If plants are also included in the set-up, they will require additional lighting more appropriate to their needs. The cage should be sprayed daily, unless running water is installed – this feature lends itself very well to a planted cage containing a group of small tropical skinks. A few species, such as the green *Lamprolepis smaragdina* from the Philippines and Solomon Islands, are arboreal in habits and should be given a tall cage with branches and living plants to climb among. These tropical skinks are nearly all oviparous, although some of the *Mabuya* species, such as *M. multifasciata* give birth to small litters of live young. None of these species are regularly bred in captivity.

A most unusual genus of semi-aquatic skinks occurs in the Philippines and the northern tip of Australia. This is *Tropidophorus*, of

72. Males of the broad-headed skink, *Eumeces laticeps*, develop colourful cheeks during the breeding season.

73.   Five-lined skink, *Eumeces fasciatus*, from North America. Skinks from several other parts of the world also have blue tails.

74.   *Mabuya quinquetaeniata*, a small, active African species which bears a striking resemblance to the North American species in Plate 73.

167

which the species *T. grayi* is sometimes offered. This species grows to about 20 cm and is dark brown in colour with obscure crossbars. The scales on the back and tail are strongly keeled, producing parallel rows of prominent 'saw-tooth' ridges. Its appearance and its semi-aquatic preferences are very unlike those of other skinks and they are usually sold as 'crocodile lizards', leading to confusion with another species altogether, *Shinisaurus crocodilurus*, from China (see Chapter 21).

Tropidophorus is found alongside streams in montane rainforests. In captivity it requires a semi-aquatic set-up, with the cage divided into land and water areas. Running water would be ideal. The land area should contain bark chippings or leaf-litter and there should be pieces of bark or small logs under which the skinks can hide. Living plants are well-suited to this type of cage, but should be species which tolerate low light conditions, such as ferns. One or two branches should also be placed in the water. They do not require very much heat and a background temperature of 20°C is probably sufficient, but there should be opportunities to bask during the day. It is not known whether ultra-violet light is necessary but the installation of a natural spectrum fluorescent light emitting at least some ultra-violet is suggested. As far as is known, they are entirely insectivorous and will eat crickets, waxworms and spiders. Although they are known to be live-bearing, giving birth to up to six young, they are probably not bred in captivity and little else is known of their biology. This would be an interesting species for enthusiasts to work with, with the aim of contributing towards a knowledge of their biology.

Scuttling from one extreme to another, the skinks from the most arid environments include several species which are known as 'sandfish', the most typical of which is *Scincus scincus* from North Africa. This and similar species have greatly reduced limbs and spend their lives burrowing through sand dunes, coming on to the surface only at night. Even though they are rarely seen, they make interesting vivarium subjects and usually thrive if given a deep layer of fine sand and plenty of heat. A heat pad should be used to warm the sand in about half of the cage to 25–30°C and this same part of the cage should be further heated by a spotlight during the day. Although the lizards will not bask on the surface, they thermoregulate by moving about under the surface. They will eat all manner of insect food, including crickets, but are more adapted to preying on insect larvae which live in the sand. For this reason, mealworms and waxworms should be fed regularly. It is not easy to supply a powdered vitamin and mineral supplement to the lizards under these conditions and an alternative way of providing these substances should be found. One solution is to feed the insects on a potent mixture of vitamins and minerals before they are used. Suitable products are available commercially but a recipe which has worked well consists of crushed trout pellets mixed with a multivitamin power and calcium in the form of crushed cuttlefish bone in the proportions 2 parts trout pellets : 1 part multivitamin powder : 2 parts ground cuttlefish bone. The insects are placed in a small container of this food for two to three days prior to being fed to the skinks. There appear to be no records of breeding these species, which are all live-bearing.

The Berber skink, *Eumeces schneideri*, comes from North African desert regions, where it lives in burrows, often among the roots of succulent shrubs. They live in large colonies, separated from neighbouring colonies by large areas of unsuitable habitats. This species varies in coloration but the most attractive form is grey on the back and tail with scattered orange scales. These scales may form irregular crossbars. The underside is plain orange to dirty white. They grow to over 30 cm, and have large powerful heads. There are no known methods of sexing the adults. They should be kept in a large cage with a deep layer of sand. A few rocks or clay drainpipes should be partially buried in order to provide retreats and heating should be provided by means of an underfloor heat pad and a spotlight, as described for the sandfish. They eat insects, small rodents and can often be persuaded to accept canned pet food. They live for a long time in captivity but are not regularly bred.

Certain of the Mediterranean *Chalcides*, such as *C. ocellatus*, the eyed skink, are similar in their habits and requirements. They fare very well in captivity and, being smaller, do not require quite so much space. They will also eat insects and will learn to accept canned pet food. Many of these species will breed regularly in the most basic of set-ups, giving birth to small litters of young during the spring and early summer after a gestation period of about two months. It seems likely that they will produce more than one litter during a year but this has not been confirmed.

In summarising this section, this has been a very brief account of a large and widespread group of lizards. There are so many small skinks which crop up from time to time in the pet trade that it would be impossible and repetitive to attempt to cover them all. Most, if not all, species will fall into one of the main categories discussed and their requirements will conform to those of the species mentioned. One problem may be the correct identification of species offered for sale, and without this further research on their origin and natural history

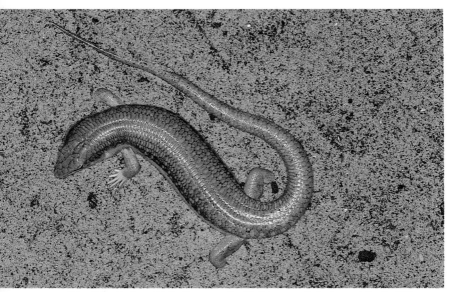

75. The Berber skink, *Eumeces schneideri*, is one of the larger North African species.

will be difficult. As a general rule, species with reduced limbs are burrowing forms but may be temperate or tropical; green skinks are arboreal and tropical; pale brown or yellowish species are likely to come from arid or semi-arid environments (and these often have reduced limbs also). When in doubt, the animals in question should be provided with a range of temperatures by heating one end of the cage. A humidity gradient should also be created by spraying one part of the cage and possibly by reducing the amount of ventilation over this area. Lighting should be by equipment which includes at least some ultra-violet. All small skinks are fairly secretive and should be provided with plenty of nooks and crannies in which they can hide, and all will eat insects of an appropriate size. Once they have settled in, preferences for certain temperatures, diets etc. can be established and the conditions modified accordingly. As it is usually difficult or impossible to distinguish the sexes superficially, a small group of, say, four or five individuals should be obtained at the outset and kept together as a colony, bearing in mind that males are sometimes territorial and must be separated if fighting occurs. Where there are individual differences in colour and markings, do not select only the most brightly coloured individuals; they will more than likely be males!

These are undemanding lizards which deserve more attention from lizard-keepers, especially in the field of breeding.

170

CHAPTER 16

Lacertids: Wall Lizards and Related Species

The family Lacertidae is exclusively Old World in distribution and contains some 200 species in 25 genera. The more frequently seen species are the small 'wall lizards', genus *Podarcis*, and the somewhat larger species from Europe and North Africa placed in the genus *Lacerta*. Several of these species are now difficult to obtain as they are protected in their countries of origin. Techniques for their successful maintenance and breeding, however, are fairly well developed and they are worth listing because a number of species are available captive-bred.

There is no doubt that, provided climatic conditions are suitable, many lacertids fare much better when kept in an outside enclosure, exposed to natural sunlight and a certain amount of natural food. Examples kept in glass vivaria indoors must be heavily supplemented with calcium and vitamin D3 if they are to survive and breed satisfactorily. Advances in equipment and a better understanding of the dietary requirements of small insectivorous lizards, however, have led to more successes, even under difficult conditions.

Large cages are required as all lacertids are lively. In addition, all of them are highly territorial; males will not tolerate other males in their vicinity and breeding groups should consist of a single male and one or more females. Unfortunately, males are usually far more colourful than females and so beginners are often lured into buying a group consisting entirely of males. In those species which do not show an obvious sexual dimorphism in coloration (very few) the larger femoral and pre-anal pores of males make their identification straightforward.

In indoor cages, heating should be provided by an overhead spotlight, which should be capable of providing a hot-spot of around 40°C. This should be positioned at one end of the cage so that the lizards can thermoregulate naturally. In addition, a fluorescent lamp which emits ultra-violet is also recommended, even when vitamin D3 is given as a dietary supplement. Both heater and light should be wired up through a time-switch and the daylength should be altered throughout the year to coincide approximately with seasonal variation. During the winter, heat can be withheld altogether, provided the temperature of the cage is not likely to fall too low. Minimum temperatures will depend on the species concerned and its natural range, but most will withstand 10°C for long periods and short spells at slightly lower temperatures. Unless these natural light and temperature cycles are simulated the lizards are unlikely to come into breeding condition in the spring.

The substrate can be of gravel or sand, depending to some extent on species, or an artificial substrate may be used. There seems to be a psychological need to dig and burrow and a substrate such as newspaper will soon lead to loss of condition. The substrate should be kept dry, although drinking water should be present at all times. One or more piles of rocks can be arranged in such a way as to provide basking surfaces on top as well as shelter underneath. Most species seem to relish an occasional spraying, provided that the humidity in the cage is not allowed to rise for too long. If potted plants are to be included, these should be of species which have little requirement for water, i.e. semi-desert species, and are best left in their pots.

Their diet consists of small insects and other invertebrates. Crickets are probably the most readily obtained live food but, whenever possible, the diet should be varied with other insects such as waxmoth larvae and mixed invertebrates which have been collected with a sweep net. Certain of the larger species may also accept young mice and some vegetable material. Large lacertids frequently eat small lacertids, so mixed communities of species which differ widely in size are not possible. It is essential to provide additional calcium and vitamin D3 in the diet of all lacertids, whether they are maintained outside or in.

Breeding begins in the spring and often continues throughout the summer, especially in the case of small species. At this time the females, especially, benefit from ample calcium in order to form their eggs. Clutches are laid in damp sand and this should be provided in a separate container in inside cages. Outside enclosures should incorporate a sandy area for egg-laying and this should be positioned in such a way that it gains maximum benefit from the sun's rays throughout the day. The eggs are removed from the sand for artificial incubation in moist sand or vermiculite at a temperature of about 28°C.

Hatchlings will only survive and grow properly if their diet is carefully supplemented. Temperatures for juveniles should not be

76. The spiny-footed lizard, *Acanthodactylus erythrurus*, a small lacertid from southern Europe and North Africa.

allowed to fall below 15°C. Otherwise their care is much as for adults. They can be housed in fairly dense groups to start with but as they grow they require progressively more room. Once sexual maturity is reached it will be necessary to separate the males from one another.

Representative species

Only a sample can be given. Very many species and subspecies are potentially available, although in many cases only occasionally. For our purposes they are most conveniently divided into large and small species.

The small species include all those at present placed in the genera *Podarcis*, *Psammodromus*, *Acanthodactylus*, *Takydromus* and others, as well as a number of the smaller members of the genus *Lacerta*.

The spiny-toed lizards, genus *Acanthodactylus*, are mainly North African although one species, *A. erythrurus*, also occurs in the Iberian peninsula. These species are adapted to living in arid regions, often around the fringes of deserts. They average about 20 cm in total length and are usually grey with paler stripes and/or blotches. Care and breeding are as in the family description, although these species probably require higher temperatures than the European wall lizards and the temperature during hibernation should be maintained at around 12°C. Clutches of 1–6 eggs are laid throughout the summer. These hatch after an incubation period of about 40 days at a temperature of 28°C.

77. The European viviparous or common lizard, *Lacerta vivipara*, a good candidate for outdoor vivaria in cooler parts of the world.

78. *Podarcis muralis*, one of several small lacertids known as 'wall' lizards.

79. *Podarcis pityusensis*, just one of the small lacertids from the Balearic Islands.

A few members of the genus *Lacerta* are small enough to be included in this section. The best known of these is the European common lizard, or viviparous lizard, *L. vivipara*. This small species grows to about 15 cm in total length. It has rather dull coloration in comparison with many other lacertids, but has the distinction of being the only viviparous species and by far the hardiest. Basically brown in colour, males are usually spotted with black, some of these spots having light centres. Females are usually striped, or have spots arranged longitudinally, and the juveniles are dark brown, almost black. This species should be kept outdoors or in a cool place indoors. Although it likes to bask, consistently high temperatures do not suit it. It is more secretive than most other lacertids and likes to forage amongst dead leaves, fragments of bark and so on. Females produce only one brood of 4–10 young in late summer after a gestation period of two to three months.

The Caucasian rock lizard, *Lacerta saxicola*, and a few other related species of small lacertids are unusual in being parthenogenetic: females are able to lay fertile eggs without ever having mated. This trait has also evolved independently in several other lizard families, notably among the whiptail lizards of the family Teiidae. *Lacerta saxicola* is a fairly drab species which lives amongst rocks and is flattened as an adaptation to hiding in crevices. Although it is not

175

widely kept in captivity it can be treated in the same manner as other wall lizards, with the 'advantage' that males are unnecessary for breeding to take place. Males of this species do exist, however, but are extremely rare. Conventional (i.e. sexual) reproduction results in offspring of both sexes, but parthenogenetic reproduction results in female offspring only. Small clutches of two or three eggs are laid throughout the summer.

Podarcis muralis, the common wall lizard, is a typical small lacertid, growing to a total length of about 20 cm and occurring in a variety of colour variations, many of which have subspecific status. Specimens from Central Europe tend to be mainly brown, whereas those from Southern Europe are often more colourful. For instance, *P. muralis brueggmanni* from Italy is bright green with a network of black reticulations covering its back and flanks. Males are invariably brighter than females, dorsally and ventrally. This species is usually fairly hardy in captivity and is an ideal subject for outdoor enclosures (small feral populations have even established themselves in several parts of Britain). Small clutches of 3–6 eggs are laid throughout the summer.

Podarcis sicula, the ruin lizard, is slightly larger than the preceding one and less variable. Most individuals are green, with a vertebral stripe of brown with black spots. The flanks are beige with black markings. Females are similarly marked but their coloration is less intense.

Two species and many subspecies of brightly coloured wall lizards occur on the Balearic Islands in the Mediterranean. *Podarcis pityusensis* is the Ibizan wall lizard, a highly variable species, populations of which are found on almost every islet and emergent rock off the coasts of Ibiza and Formentera, and numerous subspecies have been named. This is a large and robust wall lizard which may be green, blue or black in basic colour. The blue and green forms have variable black markings on their back and flanks and may be white, yellow or orange beneath. The population on the small islet of Vedra, *P. pityusensis vedrae*, is a stunning bright blue colour and could well be the world's most brightly marked lizard. The black forms come from melanistic populations and often have deep blue undersides. Hatchlings of these forms are lighter in colour and have markings similar to those of other subspecies, but gradually darken as they mature. Care and breeding are as in the family description. All forms are generally tough and undemanding in captivity.

Lilford's wall lizard, *Podarcis lilfordi*, parallels *P. pityusensis* on and around the other two Balearic Islands, Majorca and Menorca. Again, the colours and markings are highly variable and numerous subspecies

80. A juvenile Algerian racer, *Psammodromus algirus* , a species which is also found in southern Iberia.

81. Male *Takydromus sexlineatus*, a small Asian lacertid with an unusually long tail. The female is less boldly striped. This species appears to adapt well to captivity but is not regularly bred.

are recognised. The nominate race, *P. lilfordi lilfordi* is melanistic, even as a juvenile. This is one of the most hardy wall lizards, and will live for many years in captivity. They will eat a certain amount of vegetation, including fruit and vegetables, as well as insects, and well-fed examples have swollen tails; this acts as a food storage organ. Males are not as aggressive towards one another as are those of most other lacertids. Small clutches of relatively large eggs are laid.

The *Psammodromus* species are found in North Africa and the Iberian peninsula. They differ from *Podarcis* in having heavily keeled scales, giving them a somewhat spiky appearance. *P. algirus* is brown in colour with four white or yellow longitudinal stripes. It grows to about 25 cm in total length.

P. hispanicus is smaller, about 12 cm in total length, and may be grey or brown in colour. The markings consist of longitudinal rows of dark spots, sometimes running into each other to form stripes. Occasional specimens are without markings.

Takydromus sexlineatus, the six-lined takydromus, is by far the most frequently offered species of Asian lacertid as it is imported in large numbers and distributed through the pet trade. *Takydromus* is an extremely slender lacertid, with a greatly elongated tail; this can

178

82. Schreiber's lizard, *Lacerta shreiberi*, is a large and attractive lacertid from southern Europe which is closely related to the more common green lizard and can be cared for in the same way.

account for over three-quarters of its total length, which reaches about 30 cm. The male has a bronze back, and a dark brown line running down either flank. The lower flanks are pure white. Females have a similar arrangement of lines but the colours are less bright and the markings less distinct. These interesting lizards have a wide range across central and southern Asia and apparently inhabit grassy plains. In captivity they climb fairly well. They should be kept warm throughout the year, although a slight temperature drop in winter would probably do no harm, and fed on small insects. The females lay small clutches of 2-3 eggs, but there appear to have been no serious attempts to breed them regularly.

The larger lacertids are placed in the genera *Lacerta* and *Gallotia*. A group of some six or seven species of *Lacerta* are sometimes known collectively as green lizards. The *Gallotia* species, from the Canary Islands, are of a similar size. All are colourful species, most of which have been bred in captivity on a limited but regular basis. Their requirements are similar to those outlined under the family description but due to their size these species require larger cages, preferably large outdoor enclosures. Many of them will eat small vertebrates such as young mice as well as insects and, on occasion, vegetable material.

Gallotia galloti and *G. stehlini* occur on the Canary Islands, along with one or two other, less common species. They reach a total length of about 35 cm and both species are brown or olive in colour. Males have large black heads, blue throats and jowls and several blue areas on the flanks. Females are paler brown in colour and have darker longitudinal stripes. These are amongst the more aggressive species and should be housed in pairs. Their general maintenance and breeding is as in the family description but their diet can include fruit, vegetables and even canned pet food. Females lay clutches of 3–6 eggs during the summer and these hatch in 40–60 days.

Lacerta lepida, the eyed lizard or jewelled lizard, is the largest and most impressive lacertid, with a total length approaching 75 cm. Eyed lizards are found in southern Europe and North Africa. They are basically green in colour but have a series of large, blue eye-spots along each flank. Males are more brightly marked than females and have much larger heads when adult. The juveniles are totally different, being brown or green with black-edged white spots over the body. There is a totally black (melanistic) form of this species which is also bred in captivity. This species needs a very large cage or enclosure. It will usually eat small mice readily, and can give a painful bite. At least two clutches can be laid each year by a single female and these range from 10–20 eggs. The hatchlings are large, about 10 cm in length, and easily reared if an adequate diet is provided.

Lacerta viridis, the European green lizard, grows to about 40 cm or more and is overall green in colour. Males are usually unmarked except for a fine stippling of black over emerald green. Females may also be uniformly coloured but often have a pair of light, longitudinal stripes running down the back. These differences are not totally consistent, however, and the sexes should be confirmed by checking the femoral pores. Adult males also have larger heads and thicker, more powerful, necks, and their throats are blue, especially during the breeding season. *Lacerta trilineata*, the Balkan green lizard is a larger version of the green lizard, growing to 50 cm in total length. It also differs in being slightly more heavily built and the breeding males have a yellow throat.

Both of these green lizards fare very well in captivity provided that they are given adequate space and a suitable diet. They are among the more prolific species of lacertid, with two or more clutches averaging around 15 eggs per clutch laid each summer. Females therefore require large quantities of calcium and vitamin D3. Breeding is most successful if they are kept in outdoor enclosures.

CHAPTER 17

Tegus, Ameivas and Racerunners

The family Teiidae contains about 225 species of small to large lizards and is restricted to the New World. Of the larger species, the two species of tegus, *Tupinambis*, grow to about one metre in length and are impressive predators, feeding on rodents and other small mammals and birds as well as carrion and some plant material. Two species of dragon lizards, *Dracaena*, are almost as large but are specialised feeders on molluscs and are hardly ever seen in captivity. The remainder of the family comprises the small diurnal insectivorous species belonging to the genus *Cnemidophorus*, and variously known as racerunners or whiptails, and several small genera of medium-sized lizards such as those belonging to the genera *Ameiva*, *Kentropyx* and *Teius*, which are mainly insectivorous but also take some carrion and vegetable material.

The racerunners closely parallel the European lacertids in appearance and habits, even down to the presence of a number of parthenogenetic species: thirteen species, living in Mexico and the southern United States, consist solely of females, which reproduce without the need to mate.

As a rule, teiids do not make good vivarium subjects. The medium-sized species are nervous and aggressive and can rarely be induced to calm down in captivity. Although some of them are quite colourful, most are brown. If they are to be kept successfully they require large cages, heated to 25–30°C, with a hot-spot of 40°C and an ultra-violet light source. A substrate of gravel is satisfactory and there should be a pile of rocks or driftwood for basking on and hiding amongst. Food consists of large insects such as crickets and locusts and this should be fortified with a vitamin and mineral preparation. Males of these species are usually more colourful and may have larger heads than the females. They are highly territorial and will not tolerate a second male in the same cage. All species are egg-laying but captive-breeding is rare.

The smaller species are rather more adaptable to captivity and can be dealt with in the same way as the small lacertids they closely resemble. Temperature and general cage set-up can be the same as those suggested for the medium-sized species, but their food should consist of smaller items. Males and females can be difficult to differentiate in certain species although in many, notably the tropical species such as rainbow lizard, *Cnemidophorus lemniscatus*, the males are more colourful.

Other species which may be available spasmodically are mostly North American and include the six-lined racerunner, *Cnemidophorus sexlineatus*, which is brown with six cream longitudinal lines running down its back and has greenish flanks, and the western whiptail, *C. tigris*, which is large, growing to a total length of 30 cm or more and has its dorsal stripes broken up into a series of blotches. Many of the striped racerunners are difficult to identify unless their exact origin is known; most are common but have very restricted ranges.

83. The desert grassland whiptail, *Cnemidophorus uniparens*, belongs to a small group of parthenogenetic teiids.

84. Common tegu, *Tupinambis teguixin*, a large and powerful teiid species which only rarely tames down sufficiently to make a good pet.

Breeding is rarely achieved in captivity although there is some interest in the parthenogenetic species. These have the advantage of not being territorial and so a number of individuals can be kept together in a suitable cage. They require access to ultra-violet light, preferably a blacklight, and plenty of vitamins and minerals, especially calcium. Parthenogenetic species which may be available occasionally include the Chihuahuan whiptail, *C. exsanguis*, of which there is at least one long-term laboratory colony in existence, and the desert grassland whiptail, *C. uniparens*, from southern Arizona.

The two largest species, *Tupinambis teguixin* and *T. rufescens*, both known as tegus, are spectacular species better suited to large cages in zoos rather than the average private collection. Both grow to over one metre in length and are bulky, powerful and often aggressive. Adults require cages at least two metres long and with the most basic of furnishings – a substrate of newspaper, a large water bowl and a log for basking are all that is practicable. Background temperature should be in the region of 25–30°C and a spotlight or heat-lamp should produce a hot-spot of 40°C during the day. Tegus are scavengers and can be fed on dead rodents, chicks or canned pet food. Their appetites are large, and they are not the easiest of animals to keep clean. Although they will usually learn to take food from their keeper, they nearly always resent handling and will give a painful bite if provoked. They must therefore be handled with care, taking a firm grip around the neck with one hand while supporting the body with the other. The tail can be tucked under one arm. It may be necessary for two people to co-operate when handling large truculent individuals.

Males have obvious femoral pores and broad heads. Older animals develop large jowls. They are aggressive towards each other and fights often result in serious wounds. Breeding activity sometimes occurs during the summer and at this time males are especially aggressive. Once mating activity has ceased the pair must be separated. Clutches of 5–10 eggs are laid in a damp substrate such as sand or peat but these rarely hatch in captivity.

CHAPTER 18

Alligator Lizards, Legless Lizards and Galliwasps

The 75 species included in the family Anguidae have a wide distribution over Europe, Asia and North and South America. A number of species are also found in the West Indies. Although they are a fairly varied group, they have several characteristics which link them. They have thick, shiny scales, a tendency to have reduced or absent limbs and may have a fold of skin along each flank. All species are likely to discard their tail if they are grabbed roughly. Each genus has its own collective common name.

Many of these species make good choices for the vivarium although few are colourful. They share with the skinks the advantage of requiring very little vitamin D3 with little need for ultra-violet radiation, and are therefore not so prone to the same deficiencies as many other captive lizards. Because they differ somewhat in size and captive requirements they are dealt with in groups of similar species.

The alligator lizards are among the most familiar. These are classified into two genera, *Gerrhonotus* and *Elgaria*. They occur in North and Central America and are often common in suitable habitats. These species have heavily armoured bodies, long sinuous tails and short legs. When moving rapidly through dense vegetation the limbs are laid along the sides of the body and play no part in locomotion. When climbing, the tail may be used as a counterbalance or it may act as a fifth limb. Although they come from arid regions, they tend to be found alongside streams and in other humid micro-habitats, hiding beneath logs, or in bushes or tussocks of grass.

In captivity, they require medium-sized cages with plenty of cover. A substrate of dead leaves seems to suit them very well and this should be scattered with several fragments of bark to provide hiding places. Some twiggy branches or, better still, one or two tough pot plants such as ivy, will provide perches and give the lizards something to climb over. These lizards are very cold-tolerant and may also be kept in

85. Arizona alligator lizard, *Elgaria kingii*.

outside enclosures. A daytime temperature of about 25°C is sufficient, although a spotlight can be directed towards one part of the cage to allow thermoregulation to take place. A fluorescent light should be installed, preferably one producing some ultra-violet. They are insectivorous and will eat crickets, waxworms, mealworms, etc. These should be dusted with a vitamin/mineral supplement and breeding females, especially, should receive extra calcium in the form of powdered egg-shell or cuttlefish bone.

Most alligator lizards lay eggs but the northern species, *Elgaria coeruleus*, gives birth to about 12 live young. In all species, the males have wider heads than the females and are territorial: only one can be kept in each cage or enclosure. Mating takes place in the spring and during copulation the male grips the female's neck in his jaws. In oviparous species, the eggs are laid about two months later and number 10–20 per clutch. In some forms, e.g. *E. multicarinatus*, and possibly in all, the female constructs a nest chamber in damp sand or soil, often beneath a large flat rock if one is available. After laying the clutch she coils around the eggs and protects them during the incubation period. This degree of parental care is only found among

86.   The Texas alligator lizard, *Gerrhonotus liocephalus*, is one of the larger members of the family.

alligator lizards and some of the skinks from the same part of the world – an interesting coincidence. The eggs can be removed to be incubated artificially as described in Chapter 7, or, if disturbance can be avoided, they can be left with the mother. They hatch in just over one month at a temperature of 28–30°C. The hatchlings measure about 10 cm in total length and begin to feed straight away. As they grow they may require dividing up into groups of similar sized individuals as they can be aggressive towards one another. A plentiful source of vitamins and calcium is important and exposure to ultra-violet would almost certainly be beneficial. Growth is steady if they are fed well and the young lizards will become sexually mature in their second year. Newborn young of *G. coeruleus* are of a similar size and can be reared equally easily.

Although the two species referred to above are the ones most commonly seen in captivity, several others may be available occasionally. These include the Arizona alligator lizard, *Elgaria kingii*, a very pretty species which is beige above with broad irregular bands of black and brick red across the back and tail. It is the most slender species and has a particularly long tail. The Texas alligator lizard, *Gerrhonotus liocephalus*, is a large species, sometimes approaching 50 cm in total length, and with a large powerful head. It is brown or putty-coloured above with brown crossbands of light and dark scales across the back. Both these species can be cared for as described above.

Members of the genus *Ophisaurus* are known as glass lizards, owing to the readiness with which they part with their tail. They are found in North America, Europe and Asia. All lack limbs and have long cylindrical bodies and elongated tails. The other legless species mentioned here is the slow-worm, *Anguis fragilis*, a small species from Europe and western Asia.

These species can be cared for in much the same manner as the alligator lizards but, as they vary in size, cages much be chosen accordingly. Several species can be maintained successfully in outside enclosures. All are secretive, and are rarely found abroad during the heat of the day. Their cages should contain a deep layer of leaf-litter in which they can burrow and plenty of dead leaves, bark and rotten wood amongst which they can hide. A temperature of 25–30°C is satisfactory for all except the slow-worm, which should be kept cooler. A spotlight may be used to create a basking area but this should not be too powerful. The cages should be sprayed occasionally to maintain a reasonably high humidity, although the substrate should not be allowed to become too wet and the atmosphere in the cage should not become stagnant.

87. Eastern glass lizard, *Ophisaurus ventralis*, a legless anguid.

These species will eat insects and other soft-bodied invertebrates, such as earthworm, slugs and snails. The large European glass lizard, *Ophisaurus apodus*, is especially fond of the latter. All *Ophisaurus* species can usually be trained to accept raw meat or canned pet food, remembering to add plenty of vitamins and calcium. Be warned that these species will also eat smaller lizards if they are housed with them.

Breeding does not often take place in captivity, the main reason being lack of interest in the species. It can be difficult to distinguish the sexes in the *Ophisaurus* species although males may develop broader heads and large jowls with age. Mating takes place in the spring and clutches of eggs vary from 4–20 in number, depending on species and on the age of the female. In North American species, the eggs are normally guarded by the females, but may be removed for artificial incubation in captivity. As far as is known, European and Asian species of glass lizards do not show parental care of this kind and artificial incubation is necessary. The slender young measure 12–15 cm in total length. The hatchlings' colours and markings are often different from those of the adults. Rearing them presents no problems provided vitamins and calcium are added to their food.

One of the species most likely to be met with is the large European glass lizard, *Ophisaurus apodus*, which grows to well over a metre in length, of which the tail accounts for three-fifths. Adults are dark brown with paler heads and underparts. Juveniles are greenish grey with distinct dark crossbars of chocolate brown and their scales are strongly keeled, forming numerous longitudinal ridges down the back. The two most common North American species are the eastern glass lizard, *O. ventralis*, and the slender glass lizard, *O. attenuatus*. These are extremely similar to one another but may be distinguished by the presence of dark stripes above and below the lateral fold in *O. attenuatus*, but only above the fold in *O. ventralis*. The Asian species are almost never seen in captivity.

The remaining legless anguid is the slow-worm, *Anguis fragilis*. This is a common reptile in most parts of Europe except the hot, dry southern parts. In this species the males are uniformly brown in colour whereas the females and juveniles are coppery above with dark flanks and a thin dark vertebral stripe. This species gives birth to live young. Mating takes place in the spring and the females produce litters of 6–12 young in late summer. Slow-worms have been known to live for more than fifty years in captivity.

Of the remaining genera, only *Diploglossus* is likely to be of interest to lizard-keepers. Several species are found in the West Indies and Central America and are commonly known as galliwasps. The giant Haitian species, *D. warreni*, is kept and bred quite successfully in captivity. This species grows to 50 cm or more in length, the males being longer and having much broader heads. They will eat large insects readily and also accept small rodents. This species should have its cage sprayed daily as it requires rather more humidity than the glass lizards. It requires a temperature of 25–30°C, and a spotlight should be used to elevate this slightly at one end of the cage. Mating takes place in the spring and the young are born live during the summer. Litters range from 20–35 young. These can be reared in groups and will accept small insects and chopped rodents. Many can only be induced to start feeding by offering pieces of fish and then scenting other items with this for the first two or three feeds.

Anguids which are rarely seen include an interesting arboreal genus, *Abronia*, from Central America. These lizards are apparently restricted to the forest canopy where they live amongst epiphytic bromeliad plants. They have long prehensile tails but little appears to be known about their natural history or their requirements in captivity.

CHAPTER 19

Girdle-tailed Lizards, Plated Lizards and Related Species

The family Cordylidae, with over 50 species of small to fairly large lizards, is restricted to Africa and Madagascar. Several groups of species can be recognised. The girdle-tailed lizards, placed in the genus *Cordylus*, are heavily armoured with pointed scales and a spiny tail; the plated lizards, *Gerrhosaurus* and related genera, have large plate-like scales and a fold of skin along their flanks; the rock lizards are placed in the genera *Platysaurus* and *Pseudocordylus*, are more or less flattened from top to bottom and have large scales arranged in a series of rings around their tails although these are not spiny; and the snake lizards, genus *Tetradactylus*, are very elongated and have greatly reduced limbs, sometimes with the front limbs absent altogether.

Care of these species varies slightly, and some are more difficult in captivity than others, but their basic requirements are similar. They require roomy cages of varying size, according to the species. These should be kept dry and warm, with a background temperature of 25–30°C in the summer and a spotlight or heat-lamp producing a hot-spot of at least 40°C during the day. Day and night-time temperatures can be allowed to fall slightly during the winter. A powerful blacklight appears to be essential to keep these species in good health and this should be arranged so that the lizards are exposed to it while they are basking in the heat from the spotlight. Additional lighting, for instance from a natural spectrum fluorescent tube, is also important as these species like bright conditions. Equally important is the addition of vitamins and minerals to their diet.

A number of species in this family are no longer as freely available as they were formerly. The *Cordylus* species in particular are rare and are now protected over most of their collective range (southern Africa) and are almost never seen. This is unfortunate because this genus contains such interesting species as the sungazer, *Cordylus giganteus*, a large species which lives in grasslands and has a territory centred

191

88.   Giant zonure, or sungazer, *Cordylus giganteus*, from southern Africa.

around a long burrow which it excavates, and the armadillo lizard, *C. cataphractus*, a heavily armoured species which grips its tail in its mouth in order to present a thorny hoop when molested.

A substrate of gravel is appropriate for most of these species and, since most of them live around rocky outcrops, a pile of large flat rocks, with crevices between them, will provide the hiding places which are important to their sense of security. A few robust succulent plants, such as Aloes and Haworthias, positioned in the shade of the rocks, will add aesthetically to the set-up although they are by no means essential to the lizards. The two largest species, *Cordylus giganteus* and *C. warreni* grow to 40 cm and 30 cm respectively and so they need large cages, at least one metre in length and half a metre in width. Both these species will eat small rodents as well as insects. Like all *Cordylus*, the males have larger femoral pores than the females but are otherwise indistinguishable. They appear not to be territorial and a group of mixed sexes will live together with only a loose social hierarchy.

Breeding in captivity is not commonplace in Europe or North America – one problem with South African species is the reversal of the seasons when they are moved to the northern hemisphere, but other factors may also be responsible. In nature they give birth to small litters of live young: one or two in *C. giganteus* and up to six in the other species.

Members of the genera *Platysaurus* are strongly associated with rock outcrops. They are greatly flattened from top to bottom, an adaptation to living between flakes of weathered rock, and although they may measure over 30 cm in length they are only about 1 cm thick. Males of these species are much more brightly coloured than the females and can be distinguished at a glance; most have an orange tail and a green body, while the throat and underside of the body is brilliant electric blue. By contrast, the females and juveniles are brown with longitudinal cream stripes or rows of spots. The ten species vary only slightly in appearance and most have very localised distributions. They can all be treated as described for the small, rock dwelling *Cordylus* species. They are primarily insectivorous but may also eat small quantities of plant material, especially flowers. All species lay two elongated eggs but captive breeding outside their natural range is almost unheard of.

The five species of *Pseudocordylus* are known as crag lizards. They are also rock-dwellers and are intermediate in appearance between the girdle-tailed lizards and the flat lizards, being not so heavily armoured as the former nor as flattened as the latter. Males are again more brightly coloured than females and are aggressively territorial. The largest species, *P. microlepidotus*, grows to 35 cm but they are all fairly similar in appearance. Males have orange or yellow flanks and underparts and this colour extends on to the tail in the form of blotches. The head, dorsal surface and tail are brown. Females are brown with indistinct paler, mottled markings. Their care is as described for the other members of the family. Females give birth to 1–4 live young.

The plated lizards, genus *Gerrhosaurus*, are placed in a different sub-family from the genera listed above. They are medium to large species with a fold along each flank, and squarish scales arranged in rows across and along the back. Most species are basically brown in colour although stripes may be present on the back. The two species most often seen in captivity are among the largest: the tawny, or rough-scaled plated lizard, *G. major*, and the giant plated lizard, *G. validus*. These grow to a total length of about 50 cm and 70 cm respectively.

All plated lizards require a hot, dry environment. Background heating should give a daytime temperature of 25–30°C and a spotlight

89.   Warren's girdled lizard, *Cordylus warreni*, one of the more colourful members of the genus.

should produce a hot-spot of 35–40° C. Temperatures can be allowed to fall slightly at night. Ultra-violet light in the form of a blacklight should also be provided. Sand and gravel are suitable substrates and the cage should be furnished with a large pile of rocks into which the lizards can retreat. The smaller species are more or less exclusively insectivorous but the two large species mentioned above will also accept small rodents, some vegetable material and canned pet food. All food should be fortified with a vitamin and mineral supplement, including extra calcium if breeding is to be attempted.

Males of some species, e.g. *Gerrhosaurus major*, have larger femoral pores than the females but the sexes of other species, such as *G. validus*, are difficult to distinguish; males may become slightly more colourful during the breeding season, especially around the jowls and throat. These species appear to show little territorial aggression and breeding groups can be maintained together throughout the year, with

90.   *Platysaurus guttatus*, one of several colourful flat lizards.

careful monitoring to ensure that individuals at the bottom of the
pecking order are not overly harassed. In the northern hemisphere,
mating takes place in the early spring and small clutches of eggs are
laid in a damp substrate, which must be provided in a large container
for this purpose. The incubation period lasts for about two months at
a temperature of 30°C and the hatchlings are relatively large compared
to the adults. The young can be maintained in the same way as the
adults and rearing them should present few problems.

   Of the remaining six genera in this family, the two from
Madagascar, *Tracheloptychus* and *Zonosaurus*, are similar to *Gerrhosaurus* and can be maintained in a similar way, although they are rarely
kept in captivity. *Angolosaurus* is a specialised plated lizard which lives

195

91.   Rough-scaled plated lizard, *Gerrhosaurus major*.

in sand dunes in much the same way as the sandfish of North Africa (see Chapter 15); it is unlikely to become freely available to collectors. The small *Tetradactylus* and *Chamaesaura* species are not rock-dwellers, living instead among low vegetation; they should be given roomy cages with a substrate of sand or fine gravel, covered with a layer of dead leaves, grasses or bracken and a few flat stones to hide beneath. All species are insectivorous and will eat the usual selection of insects, dusted generously with vitamins and calcium. They lay small clutches of eggs but their breeding biology is not well known. *Cordylosaurus* is a brightly coloured dwarf plated lizard from desert regions in southwest Africa, where it lives among rocks. Its natural history is little known and it has probably not been kept in captivity.

CHAPTER 20

Chameleons

The chameleons are, without a doubt, the most fascinating and spectacular lizards. Their unmistakable shape, swivelling eyes, bizarre feeding habits and exaggerated ability to change colour have all contributed to their popular appeal, while their slow deliberate gait and usually docile temperament have lured many people into purchasing and attempting to maintain them. Unfortunately, chameleons are amongst the most demanding lizards to care for and the overwhelming majority of those collected for the pet trade perish within weeks or months. Any ambitions to keep these species, therefore, must be accompanied by a commitment to much time and effort in creating the correct conditions and supplying a varied and plentiful diet.

Chameleons are, of course, highly arboreal. Their anatomical adaptations – the prehensile tail, opposed digits and leaf-like shape – have all evolved as a direct result of this specialisation. Their cage, therefore, should be tall enough to contain large growing plants, preferably in pots. Dead branches should also be included as these will provide perches on which the lizards will spend most of their time and on which they will sleep. Chameleons have a large space requirement and will suffer stress if kept in a cage which is too small. Some of the best breeding results have come from colonies which have been allowed free run of a room or conservatory or, in warmer parts of the world, an outside 'aviary' type of cage. Indoor cages should be a minimum of one cubic metre, whether a single animal, pair or small colony is to be kept. The very large species, such as several of those from Madagascar, require cages well in excess of this size, while the more territorial species would require huge cages if they were to be housed together (which is therefore not advisable). Cages can be made to appear more spacious to the occupants if they are entirely of glass, although glass cages containing territorial chameleons should not be placed next to one another.

Temperatures will depend on the species to be kept and its origin although, in general, the species which are most commonly available tend to prefer rather cool conditions, about 25–30°C. Note that most chameleons are forest species and rarely seem to thermoregulate: if part of the cage is too cold, an individual finding itself there may not have the instinct to seek out a warmer position. Nevertheless, a spotlight should be directed to one part of the cage during the day so that individuals preferring an occasional higher temperature can be accommodated.

Few chameleons will drink from a water dish and so the plants and sides of the cage should be sprayed heavily at least once each day. An alternative is to arrange a small trickle of running water, producing a spray which collects into droplets on leaves. Chameleons which become dehydrated have sunken eyes and can be difficult to revive. Persuading healthy chameleons to feed is rarely a problem, at least in the beginning. For such a slow-moving animal, their appetites are large and they will often take huge quantities of food. This can consist of cultured insects such as crickets and locusts (especially for the larger species) and waxmoth larvae. Cockroaches are a useful additional item if available, either cultured or captured, as are any other large insects which can be collected without risk of chemical contamination. Large species will also eat young rodents such as nestling mice and rats, and all species prey on smaller lizards. A constant supply of food is vital; a well-fed chameleon will refuse food once it is replete but will often be ready for another meal a few hours later. A day or two without food will cause a dramatic loss of condition. Even if a good variety of food is offered, chameleons which do not have access to sunlight will require vitamin supplements, which can be given in liquid form through an eye dropper or as a powder sprinkled on to their food. Vitamin D3 and calcium are the most important requirements and several suitable products are designed specifically for reptiles.

Chameleons are highly territorial and they are less trouble to maintain if kept individually except at breeding time. On the other hand, social interactions and displays are one of the most fascinating aspects of keeping them and there is no reason why a small group cannot be kept together in harmony provided a few simple precautions are taken. As a rule, males, which are easily recognisable by their horns, crests or other embellishments, should not be kept together in the same cage or even within sight of each other if they are in separate cages. If a male is kept with a group of females a spare cage should be available in order to segregate the male if he becomes aggressive towards the female(s) but this normally occurs only during the

92. Male sailfin chameleons, *Chamaeleo montium*, are easily distinguishable by their very obvious horns. Many other species also have head ornamentation.

breeding season. Where a group of animals is kept together it will be necessary to ensure that each one is receiving an adequate amount of food; some animals may become dominant and prevent the others from feeding, either by getting to the food first every time or by causing them to cringe away submissively in some dark corner of the cage.

Successful breeding has only been achieved by those people prepared to invest much time and effort in their animals. The conditions for their maintenance must be as near to perfect as possible and there must be a good understanding of their behavioural requirements as well as their physiological needs.

Chameleons may be oviparous or viviparous, depending on species. Both kinds are equally easy (or difficult) to breed although the oviparous species also require some expertise in incubating eggs. Breeding animals must be in first-class condition, otherwise the females will not withstand the added stress of producing eggs or young, especially as they often refuse to feed immediately prior to egg-laying or birth. Males and females of most species come into breeding condition as a result of increased daylength, and this can be manipulated artificially if the cages do not receive plenty of natural light. Males show enhanced coloration at this time and may become aggressive, especially to other males if present, but also to females. Females of live-bearing species may be separated when they are obviously pregnant but this may not be necessary if there is plenty of food in the cage at all times. Furthermore, the stress caused by moving them may be counterproductive. Females of oviparous species must be given a suitable site in which to lay their eggs and this can consist of a partitioned area on the floor of the cage or a separate egg-laying box. In either case, about six inches of peat, or peat mixed with chopped sphagnum, should be available for the female to bury her eggs. This substrate must be kept moist prior to laying and should therefore be sprayed at least once each day. The egg-laying site should be in a shaded part of the cage to prevent rapid drying out and also to give the female seclusion during egg-laying. The eggs are buried in a pit which the female excavates and they should be removed for artificial incubation as described in Chapter 7. Incubation times are very extended in nature, often one year, but should be shorter under constant conditions.

Rearing the young may present something of a problem owing to their small size and high food requirement. They need plenty of space and a matrix of small twigs on which to climb. Fruit flies, *Drosophila*, in vast numbers, are probably the best food initially because these will get to every part of the cage and the chameleons will not need to search them out, but the ventilation must then be of very fine mesh to prevent escapes. Vitamin supplements and a source of ultra-violet (either natural sunlight or a special fluorescent tube) would also appear to be vital, although very few young chameleons have been successfully reared except in large outdoor enclosures and precise information is lacking. In nature, some species at least mature within one year and so growth must necessarily be rapid under ideal conditions.

Representative species

Although numerous species have been imported into Europe and North America over the years, only a small selection can be described. Other species can be cared for as in the family description above, although some species are more easily cared for than others.

Viviparous species include the dwarf chameleons, *Bradypodion*, which comprise thirteen species, although these are not easily distinguishable unless their origin is known precisely. They are often listed collectively as *Bradypodion* (or *Chamaeleo*) *pumilum* and come from southern Africa. All are small, colourful species with a casque-like structure on top of the head, more pronounced in males than females. In addition, males are more brightly coloured, especially when displaying. These chameleons are more easily accommodated than some of the larger species and may be kept in small groups, bearing in mind the remarks about territoriality. They are also more cold-tolerant than many of the larger tropical species and may well be suitable for outdoor culture in the warmer parts of Europe and North America, at least during the spring and summer months. Females give birth to one or more broods, consisting of up to 50 young. These are very tiny and would probably present considerable difficulties in rearing. Otherwise, their care is as in the family description.

Jackson's chameleon, *Chamaeleo jacksoni*, which comes from East Africa, is unmistakable. Males have three long horns protruding from the snout, each one ringed with a series of grooves. The females lack the horns but have rudimentary thorn-like tubercles in their place. The size of this species appears to depend on its origin: apparently, the larger specimens sometimes available come from a montane population around Mount Kenya and surrounding areas, whereas the smaller specimens, growing to about 30 cm in total length, are lowland forms. This species does reasonably well in captivity, at least for a while. Its care is as described above, and breeding has been achieved on several occasions, usually following a period of warm weather when it can be kept outside in a large cage of wire mesh. Breeding takes place in the summer, with the young being born about nine months later, i.e. in late winter or spring. Litters can comprise up to 50 young, each measuring about 3 cm in total length. They are born in a thin transparent sac from which they free themselves immediately and then disperse throughout the vegetation. Use of an ultra-violet light source is probably essential for rearing but sexual maturity can be reached within one year if conditions are good.

Of the egg-laying species, the flap-necked chameleon, *Chamaeleo dilepis*, is one of the best vivarium subjects. It is a deep-bodied species from southern Africa, is normally some shade of green but may be yellow or brown. Males have a pair of flaps extending from the back of the head. This species will withstand occasional cool conditions, and usually eats readily. Females lay large clutches of 30 or more eggs and these hatch in 100–300 days depending on temperature.

The largest chameleon in the world is *Chamaeleo oustaleti*, from Madagascar. This species is not one of the more colourful, being pale to reddish brown with only faint traces of darker streaks. There is a raised casque on the top of the head, larger in the males, and it can grow in excess of 50 cm. It appears to be a tough and relatively easy species to maintain. Because of its large size it will eat small rodents

93. One of the smaller species of chameleons, *Chamaeleo lateralis*.

readily and this is undoubtedly a factor in its good performance. Large cages are obviously necessary although this species is apparently less territorial than some of the others and males will live together in harmony.

Another large Madagascan species, the panther chameleon, *Chamaeleo pardalis*, is deep-bodied and has a prominent 'saw-tooth' crest along the ridge of its back and an angled casque on the top of its head. In both sexes the top of the head is flattened and extended slightly to form a short, broad horn. Males in breeding condition may be bright blue or bluish green but at other times they are more drab. Females are brown or reddish brown. Males of this species can be kept together when not in breeding condition.

Parson's chameleon, *Chamaeleo parsoni*, is one of the more spectacular species. Males and females are bright green with reddish or orange markings. The males have a strange gnarled horn extending from their snout. The species grows to 45 cm or more and comes from Madagascar. It will readily eat small rodents.

A variety of species have been available in small numbers recently, many of them from Madagascar. Their suitability as captives is difficult to assess and beginners are advised to acquire some expertise in keeping easier species of lizards before *any* chameleon is purchased – none of them are easy and many of them are extremely difficult to maintain satisfactorily.

CHAPTER 21

The Chinese Crocodile Lizard

The Chinese crocodile lizard, *Shinisaurus crocodilurus*, is the sole Asian representative of the family Xenosauridae, the other three members being little-known lizards from Mexico. It occurs in a tiny area of central China and was rarely seen outside that country until recently. At present, it is available in small numbers and has aroused considerable interest among lizard-keepers.

This strange lizard grows to a total length of about 30 cm or more and has a blunt snout and stocky body. Its most distinctive feature is the rugose scalation and, in particular, the two rows of enlarged horny

94.   Chinese crocodile lizard, *Shinisaurus crocodilurus*.

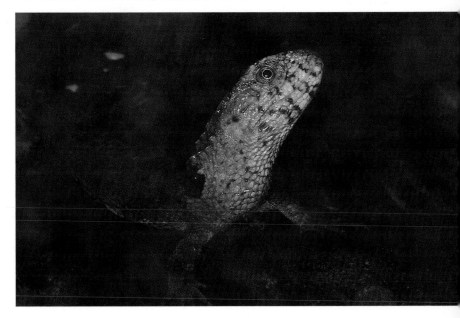

scales which run from either side of the head, down the back and on to the tail. It is this feature which has led to the lizard being likened, justifiably, to a crocodile. Furthermore, this species is semi-aquatic in habits; unlike most lizards but very like crocodiles. In colour, the crocodile lizard is drab brown, greyish-brown or olive with vague dark markings on the back and tail and three or four dark lines running from the side of the head, across the jaws and on to the chin.

This species has proven to be rather difficult to keep successfully. It appears to prefer cooler conditions than most lizards and is most happy at about 20°C. It can withstand short spells at much higher temperatures, however. The temperature should be controlled by undercage heating and a thermostat, and a spotlight is not necessary. The inclusion of a blacklight would probably be beneficial but normal lighting should be subdued. The cage should contain a large area of water, either in a dish or as an area which has been divided by a strip of glass. It must be possible to change this water regularly, either by removing the container or by siphoning. The land area should be covered with pea-gravel and there should be rocks, logs or other hiding places present. Moisture-loving plants can also be incorporated by standing their pots either in the water or plunging them into the gravel.

Although this species is widely reputed to feed on fish, tadpoles, etc. it will also accept small earthworms, waxworms and crickets, although it is not very adept at catching fast-moving prey.

Males may be slightly more colourful than females, with a watery orange suffusion over the flanks and around the throat, and a broader head. Females are often much more rotund. Captive breeding has never been reliably induced but imported females which are already pregnant may give birth to young some months after they have arrived. Litters appear to be small, often consisting of only one or two young but occasionally up to ten, and these are commonly born in the water. The newborn young measure about 12 cm in total length and are similar to the adults but rather lighter in colour. They appear to be rather difficult to rear, and may die suddenly for no apparent reason. Much work needs to be done before the requirements of this interesting and rare lizard are fully understood.

CHAPTER 22

The Gila Monster and Beaded Lizard

The small family Helodermatidae is restricted to the more arid regions of southwestern North America and northwestern Mexico and a small part of the more humid forest region in southern Mexico and neighbouring Central American countries. The two species belonging to the family, the Gila monster, *Heloderma suspectum*, and the beaded lizard, *H. horridum*, are the only venomous lizards in the world; this fact alone makes them of great interest to zoologists and to lizard-keepers. Coupled to this are a number of unusual qualities. They cannot be mistaken for any other lizards. They are covered with regularly arranged stud-like scales. Their heads are broad and flat and their snouts are bluntly rounded. The tail, which serves as a food storage organ, is thick and cylindrical. The limbs are short but powerful and are used to drag the body across the ground, giving them a rather clumsy, ponderous gait. The feet are well adapted for digging and have long claws. In colour, the Gila monster is marked with a network of black markings over a pink background. The tail is banded and the markings on the body may also be vaguely arranged into broad bands (subspecies *cinctum*). It grows to a total length of 50 cm. The beaded lizard is cream and black, with the black predominating in the majority of examples: specimens from the southern part of the range may be almost completely black (subspecies *alvarezi*). The beaded lizard is the larger of the two species and may approach one metre in total length.

The venom apparatus is situated in the lower jaw, not the upper jaw as in snakes. The venom ducts open at the base of two enlarged fangs with a sharp cutting edge and a groove up which the venom is drawn. It is worth pointing out that the venom is released into the fangs automatically every time the lizards bite; they cannot withhold venom and give a 'dry' bite in the same way that snakes can, and so every heloderm bite is dangerous. The effects of the venom are immediate

95.   Gila monster, *Heloderma suspectum.*

and extremely painful, although not often fatal. Its purpose is entirely defensive and intended to force the aggressor to withdraw, an effect which it invariably achieves.

The possession of Gila monsters and beaded lizards is controlled under the Dangerous Wild Animals Act in Britain and various other restrictions are placed on them in most other parts of the world. In

96.   Mexican beaded lizard, *Heloderma horridum*, the larger of the two venomous lizards constituting the family Helodermatidae.

addition, they are almost totally protected throughout their ranges for reasons of conservation.

These strange lizards fare well in captivity under a relatively simple regime, although breeding them has proven to be something of a challenge. Most of the information that is available relates to the Gila monster, for this is the species most commonly seen in captivity, but care and breeding of the beaded lizard probably follows much the same course.

Although they are desert lizards, their preferred body temperature is not especially high. In nature they spend most of their time below the surface, in burrows which they dig themselves or take over from other burrowing animals, emerging only during cooler weather or in the evening. For this reason, they should be provided with plenty of hiding places in the form of wooden hide-boxes or clay drainpipes. A background temperature of about 25°C is adequate during the summer, although a heat-lamp should be directed at one end of the

207

cage so that they are given the opportunity to raise their body temperatures up to 30°C or so. Usually, they will prefer to 'bask' under cover, and so at least one hide-box should be placed near to the heat-lamp. Potential breeders should be cooled down slightly during the winter. Attempts at landscaping their cage will be doomed to failure and so the set-up should be kept simple: a substrate of wood shavings or compressed sawdust pellets, a water bowl and the hiding places will suffice. There is little information on their need for ultra-violet. It seems, however, advisable to provide this, either in the form of a blacklight or a natural spectrum fluorescent tube.

Wild heloderms take a variety of animal prey, including eggs and nestling birds and rodents. They are not very adept hunters and must seek out helpless prey, using their acute sense of smell. In captivity, wild-caught heloderms are sometimes difficult to feed, and may only accept eggs. Captive-bred young, however, can easily be persuaded to eat dead rodents and this is a much more satisfactory diet than either eggs or canned pet food. The lizards will soon learn to take their food directly from (long!) feeding forceps. Vitamins, minerals such as calcium, and drugs can easily be injected or placed into a mouse carcass and this is the preferred method of administering these substances. For a desert species, their requirement for water is surprising and they will spend long periods of time soaking in a shallow bowl.

Attempts at breeding have met with mixed success. The first problem which presents itself is that of recognising the males and females. There appears to be no certain way of establishing the sexes, although various methods have been suggested, including probing and x-raying. None seems to be practical *and* reliable. Most serious breeding attempts have been initiated by the purchase of a large group of animals. These can be kept together in the breeding season and behavioural clues are then available to help identify the sexes. Intra-species aggression, even between males, appears not to be a problem, although a loose dominance hierarchy may be established. Mating takes place shortly after the animals are warmed up in the spring. At this time the lizards are far more active than usual and constantly prowl about the cage, closely investigating any other individual they encounter. It appears that only a proportion of the females will breed in any given year; this may have evolved as a method of ensuring that they have an opportunity to replenish essential food reserves and minerals between each reproduction – a number of species of snakes are known to have a similar strategy.

Some breeders advocate removing the females after mating activity

97.   Mexican beaded lizard in the process of laying an egg.

has ceased and housing them separately during egg-laying and for the remainder of the year, reintroducing them to the male(s) the following spring after hibernation. This eliminates the risk of other individuals eating the eggs after they have been laid, and may stimulate activity the following year when the animals are reintroduced. On the other hand, heloderms are colonial animals and, in the long term, a breeding group may become more productive if it is left intact. Egg-laying takes place about two months after mating and the females will require a suitable site for this. A shallow tray containing moist peat mixed with sand is placed in a quiet corner of the cage and partially covered with a board or flat rock. The female will visit this and dig around in the substrate for several days prior to egg-laying. There is also a pre-laying slough approximately three weeks before the eggs are laid.

    The eggs are large, and number 1–8. They should be removed from the egg-laying box as soon as they are discovered and incubated artificially at a temperature of 28–30°C. The substrate should be somewhat drier than is normally recommended for lizards, barely

209

moist in fact. They hatch after approximately three months. Young heloderms are much brighter in colour than the adults and are typically more aggressive than adults and can be difficult to handle. They usually feed without any problem, and will tackle small mice straight away. They will grow steadily and reach sexual maturity at three to four years of age.

CHAPTER 23

Monitors

The family of monitors, Varanidae, is widely distributed in Africa, Asia and Australasia and has a total of about 30 species, all placed in the genus *Varanus*. There are several small to medium-sized species in the genus, known as pygmy monitors, but these are all Australian and are rarely seen outside that continent. Of the larger species, the Komodo

98.   Rock, or Bosc's monitor, *Varanus exanthematicus* , from Africa. Juveniles such as this one may make attractive pets but adults require huge cages and are unlikely to breed in captivity.

dragon, *V. komodoensis*, is the world's largest lizard at a total length which may exceed four metres.

All monitors, regardless of size, have a cylindrical body, long powerful limbs, a narrow, pointed head, and a long forked tongue. The tail is long and may be used to lash out at prey or predators. In a few semi-aquatic species the tail is also flattened from side to side and is used in swimming. The scales are granular and there are often folds of skin around the throat and on the flanks. Most species are fairly drab in coloration, although juveniles may be more attractive. Although primarily terrestrial, some species are adapted for swimming and others are adept climbers. Several are associated with termite mounds, using them as retreats and for egg-laying.

All monitors are exclusively carnivorous in diet, with food items ranging from eggs, insects and small lizards in the case of several of the Australian pygmy monitors (and young of all species) to large mammals such as deer in the case of the very largest species. In addition, many of the larger species probably rely largely on carrion.

Regrettably, these magnificent lizards make very poor captives. All of the species which are freely available (*Varanus niloticus*, *V. exanthematicus* and *V. salvator*) become too large to be housed adequately by any but the most dedicated and wealthy collector. In addition, their temperament is uncertain, to say the least. Young specimens, which are frequently imported, are more colourful than adults and can be handled with a fair degree of confidence. For this reason, they appeal to beginners. As they grow, they require ever larger cages, ever more food and ever more caution when they are handled. Eventually, they become an embarrassment.

One possible exception is the arboreal species, *Varanus prasinus*. This specialised monitor from Southeast Asia is exceedingly slender and has an even more narrow head than usual. It can grow to a total length of 75 cm, of which two-thirds consists of tail. It may be bright green or black in colour, both colour forms being, apparently, equally common in places. It requires a high temperature, in the region of 30°C and humid surroundings. Its cage should be tall and should contain plenty of branches for the lizards to climb on. Food can consist of large insects, such as locusts, and small mammals. Imported specimens are likely to be heavily parasitized and should be treated accordingly.

Distinguishing the sexes of monitors by external examination is not possible. In any case, this would prove to be an academic exercise since captive breeding has not been achieved on more than one or two occasions, usually by chance, and then only in the large facilities provided by zoological gardens. The great size of these lizards precludes any possibility of normal sexual behaviour in captivity while lack of exercise and overfeeding usually results in obesity in long-term captives.

When there is such a wide variety of interesting small to medium-sized lizards available, some of them captive-bred, it is difficult to understand why the average reptile enthusiast would seriously consider the purchase of any of the large monitors.

CHAPTER 24

Amphisbaenians: Worm Lizards

The worm lizards are not, strictly speaking, lizards at all, but belong to a separate sub-order of reptiles allied to the snakes and the true lizards. Because their maintenance is unlikely to be discussed elsewhere, and because they have obvious affinities with certain types of true lizards, they are dealt with briefly here.

The 130 or so species are sub-divided into four families, but the differences between them do not concern us here. The sub-order as a whole has a distribution covering much of the tropical and sub-tropical world. With the exception of three species, they are without limbs. The three exceptions belong to the genus *Bipes* and have front limbs only. All are slender, cylindrical reptiles with blunt snouts, reinforced skulls and vestigal eyes. Their scales are arranged in a regular pattern of rings around the body, so that they look, superficially, like an earthworm. All the above characteristics are the result of their burrowing habits, and amphisbaenians spend the greater part of their lives beneath the ground. Their habitats range from dry, sandy desert regions, through grasslands and savanna to lush tropical forests. All are carnivorous and feed largely upon burrowing insects, especially their larval stages, and soft-bodied invertebrates such as earthworms. Their jaws are powerful, however, and they will tackle almost any prey of suitable size, including small rodents and lizards, given the opportunity.

Care of these species is very simple. They require several inches of a suitable substrate, the exact nature of which will depend on their natural origin, i.e. sand, sandy soil or leaf-litter. Heating should be from beneath the substrate and is most conveniently arranged by means of a heat pad – this should be positioned under half of the cage only so that the reptiles can practise a limited amount of thermoregulation. Lighting is not strictly necessary, of course, but may be installed if the cage is to be planted with appropriate material, in

99. One of the more brightly marked amphisbaenians, *Amphisbaena fuliginosa*.

100. *Trogonophis wiegmanni*, an unusual amphisbaenian from North Africa.

215

which case the plants should be left in their pots so that their roots are not disturbed by the burrowing activities of the occupants. Those species which hail from a dry environment seem to fare better if they can surface beneath a flat rock under which there is a small area of moist substrate – this can be created by lifting the rock from time to time and spraying beneath it.

Food in the form of crickets, waxworms, mealworms and earthworms should be placed in the cage regularly. The amphisbaenians will rarely be seen, but the prey will disappear gradually as they are hunted and consumed during the night, or eaten beneath the surface. The larger species, such as *Amphisbaena alba* and *A. fuliginosa*, will often accept dead rodents of the appropriate size, or even chunks of canned pet food. Other reptiles should not be kept with amphisbaenians under any circumstances.

There is little information about the private lives of these interesting reptiles and, as far as is known, it is not possible to distinguish the sexes externally. There appear to be no records of their having bred in captivity, although this is probably due to lack of trying on the part of lizard-keepers; where they are kept at all, it tends to be as curiosities, and often only a single specimen is maintained. They are not, in any case, easily obtainable. Records from wild amphisbaenians indicate that, whereas most species lay eggs, some give birth to live young.

Societies, Journals and Magazines

There are no journals or magazines dealing exclusively with lizard-keeping, but several of the amateur herpetological society publications contain relevant articles from time to time. Membership of at least one of these societies is strongly recommended. Their current addresses should be sought through local zoos, libraries and reptile dealers. The most important national and international societies, with their publications, are as follows:

Africa

Herpetological Association of Africa, Bloemfontein, South Africa.
Publication: *Journal of the Herpetological Association of Africa.*

Australasia

Australasian Federation of Herpetological Societies, Sydney, Australia.
Publication: *Herpetofauna.*

Europe

Association for the Study of Reptiles and Amphibians (ASRA), Oxford, England.
Publication: *Journal of the Association for the Study of Reptiles and Amphibians.*

British Herpetological Society (BHS), London, England.
Publications: *Bulletin of the British Herpetological Society; The Herpetological Journal.*

Deutschen Gesellschaft fur Herpetologie und Terrarienkunde, Frankfurt, Germany.
Publication: *Salamandra.*

Herpetofauna Verlags, Weinstadt, Germany.
Publication: *Herpetofauna.*

International Herpetological Society, Walsall, England.
Publication: *The Herptile.*

Nederlandse Vereniging voor Herpetologie en Terrarienkunde, Amsterdam, The Netherlands.
Publication: *Lacerta.*

United States

American Federation of Herpetoculturalists, Lakeside, California.
Publication: *The Vivarium.*

Society for the Study or Amphibians and Reptiles (SSAR), Athens, Ohio.
Publications: *Journal of Herpetology; Herpetological Review.*

In addition to those listed, there are very many local societies in Europe, North America and elsewhere, and their meetings are ideal places to meet other interested persons and to locate sources of captive-bred lizards.

Bibliography

Collections of relevant papers have been published occasionally or regularly in the following publications:

INTERNATIONAL ZOO YEARBOOK, Zoological Society of London. This annual publication often contains papers on the care and breeding of lizards. Volumes 9 and 19 each devoted a whole section to reptiles and amphibians.

PROCEEDINGS OF THE U.K. HERPETOLOGICAL SYMPOSIUM ON CAPTIVE BREEDING. Two reports have been published so far: 1986 and 1988. Both are available through the British Herpetological Society.

REPORTS OF THE INTERNATIONAL HERPETOLOGICAL SYMPOSIUM ON CAPTIVE PROPAGATION AND HUSBANDRY. These annual reports are transcripts of papers given at the symposiums, held annually at various locations in the United States.

REPTILES: BREEDING, BEHAVIOUR AND VETERINARY ASPECTS (ed. Townson and Lawrence, 1985). British Herpetological Society.

THE CARE AND BREEDING OF CAPTIVE REPTILES (ed. Townson, Millichamp, Lucas and Millwood, 1980). British Herpetological Society.

Index

All page references in *italics* refer to illustrations.

Abronia species 190
Acanthodactylus species 173
  erythrurus 173, *173*
Acanthosaura crucigera 150
Actinic (lighting) 24
Agama species 152
  agama 152
  stellio 152
Agamidae 138ff
Aleuroscalabotes felinus 69, 73
Algerian racer *177*, 178
Alligator lizards 185ff
  Arizona *186*, 188
  northern 187
  Texas *187*, 188
Amblyrhynchus cristatus 114
Ameiva species 181
Amphibolurus species see *Pogona*
Amphisbaenians 214ff
Amphisbaena alba 216
  fuliginosa 215, 216
Anarbylus switaki 77, 78
Anglosaurus 195
Anguiidae, 185ff
Anguis fragilis 188, 190
Anoles 125
  Cuban 125, *127*
  green 125, *127*
  knight 125, *126*
  large-headed 125
Anolis species, 114, 125
  carolinensis 125, *127*
  cybotes 125
  equestris 125, *126*
  sagrei 125, *127*
Armadillo lizard 192

Basiliscus species, 122
  basiliscus 123, *124*
  plumifrons 123, *123*
Basilisks 122
  brown *124*
  plumed 123, *123*

Beaded lizard 205, *207*, *209*
Bearded dragons, 142, *143*, *145*
Bipes species 214
Birth 56
Blacklight 24
Brachylophus species 114, 118
  fasciatus 119
Bradypodion species 200
Breeding 52ff
Brush lizards 129

Cages 17ff
Calcium 49, 65
Callisaurus species 132, 134
  draconoides, *133*
Calotes species 148
Chalcides species 164, 169
  ocellatus 169
Chamaeleo dilepis 201
  jacksoni 201
  lateralis 202
  montium 199
  oustaleti 201
  pardalis 202
  parsoni 202
  pumilum 200
Chamaesaura species 196
Chameleons 197ff
  dwarf 200
  flap-necked 201
  Jackson's 201
  Oustalet's 201
  panther 202
  Parson's 202
  sail-fin *199*
Chilean swifts 114, 130, *130*, *131*
Chlamydosaurus kingii 146
Chondrodactylus angulifer 94
Chuckwallas 114, 118, *119*
Cnemidophorus species 181
  exsanguis 183
  lemniscatus 182
  sexlineatus 182

tigris 182
uniparens 182, 183
Coleonyx species 69, 74
  brevis 78
  elegans 78
  mitratus 78
  reticulatus 78
  switaki 77, 78
  variegatus 75, 78
Collared lizards 132, *134*
Common lizard (European) *174*, 175
Cophosaurus species 132, 134
Cophotis ceylanica 138
Cordylidae 191ff
Cordylosaurus 196
Cordylus species 191
  cataphractus 192
  giganteus 191, 192, *192*
  warreni 192, *194*
Corucia zebrata 160, *162*
Corytophanes cristatus 126
Crag lizards 193
Crickets as food 46
Crocodile lizard, Chinese 203, *203*
Crotaphytus species 132, 134
  collaris 134
Ctenosaura species 114
Cyclura species 115
  cornuta 118
Cyrtodactylus species 87
  kotschyi 86, *87*
  pinguensis 87, *88*
  pulchellus 87

Dab lizards 138
  Egyptian 140, *141*
  Hardwick's 140
  spiny 140, *142*
Diplodactylus species 105
  ciliaris 105, *106*
  taenicauda 108
Diploglossus species 190
  warreni 190
Dipsosaurus dorsalis 121, *121*
Diseases 60ff
Disinfectants 64
Dominance hierarchies 15
Dracaena species 181
Dragon lizards 181
Dwarf geckos 87

Earless lizards 132, *133*
Egernia species 161
  cunninghami 161
  depressa 161
Egg-laying 56
Eggs 56
Elgaria species 187
  coeruleus 187, 188

kingii 186, 188
  multicarinatus 187
Entamoeba infections 67
Eublepharids 69ff
Eublepharis species 69
  macularius 61, *71*, 72, *74*
  angramainyu 73
Eumeces species 163
  fasciatus 167
  laticeps 164, *166*
  schneideri 169, *170*
Eyed lizard 180

Femoral pores 53
Fence lizards 128
  western *128*
Flat lizards 193, *195*
Flukes 66
Food 42
Frilled lizard 146
Fringe-toed lizards 132
Fruit flies 47

Galliwasps 190
  giant Haitian 190
Gallotia species 179
  galloti 180
  stehlini 180
Gambelia species 132, *134*
Geckonia chazalae 91, *92*
Geckos 79ff
  ashy 104, *104*
  banded 74, *75*, *76*
  barefoot *77*, 78
  bent-toed 87
  Brook's house 85
  day geckos 93ff
    flat-tailed *98*, 99
    Madagascan 100
    Standing's 100
    Sundberg's 100
  fat-tailed 73
  flying *83*, 84
  golden-tailed 108
  helmeted 91, *92*
  house, Asian 85
  knob-tailed *92*
  Kotschy's *86*, 87
  leopard 61, *71*, 72, *74*
  Moorish, *84*, 85
  Namib ground 93
  spiny-tailed *106*
  Turkish 85
  velvet (African) 87, *89*
  velvet (Australian) *106*
  Wahlberg's 87, *89*
  web-footed 93, *93*
  yellow-headed 105
Gekko gecko 58, 83

stentor 84
vittatus 82, 84
Gerrhonotus species 185
  liocephalus 187, 188
Gerrhosaurus species 191
  major 193, 194, 196
  validus 193, 194
Gila monster 205, 206
Girdle-tailed lizards 191
  giant 192, 192
  Warren's 192, 194
Glass lizard 189
  eastern 189, 190
  European 189
  slender 190
Gonatodes species 105
  albogularis 105
  ceciliae 105
  vittatus 103, 105
Goniurosaurus species 69
  kuroiwae 73
  lichtenfelderi 73
Green lizard, Balkan 180
  European 180

Health 60ff
Heating 21ff
Heloderma horridum 205, 207, 209
  suspectum 205, 206
Helodermatidae 205ff
Hemidactylus species 85
  brooksi 85
  turcicus 85
Hemitheconyx species 69
  caudicinctus 73
  taylori 73
Holbrookia species 132, 134
  maculata 133
Holodactylus species 69, 73
Homopholis wahlbergii 87, 89
Hoplodactylus species 108
Horned lizards 136
  round-tailed 135
  short-horned 135
Horned 'toads' 136
Humidity 25ff
Hydrosaurus pustulosus 151

Iguanas 114ff
  common 115, 115
  desert 121, 121
  Fiji 119
  ground 114, 118
  helmeted 126
  marine 114
  rhinoceros 118
Iguana species 114
  iguana 115, 115
  iguana rhinoceros 116
Iguanidae 114ff

Inbreeding 59
Incubating eggs 56
Insects as food 44

Jewelled lacerta 180

Kentropyx species 181
Komodo dragon 211

Lacerta species 171, 173, 175
  lepida 180
  saxicola 175
  schreiberi 179
  trilineata 180
  viridis 180
  vivipara 174, 175
Lacertidae 171ff
Lamprolepis smaragdina 165
Lava lizards 114
Leopard lizards 132
Lialis burtoni 110
Light cycles 23
  diurnal variations 23
  seasonal variations 23
Lighting 22ff
Liolaemus species 114, 130, 130, 131
  tenuis 130
Liolepis belliana 138
Lygodactylus species 87

Mabuya species 163, 164, 165
  multifasciata 165
  quinquetaeniata 167
Mastigures 138
  Egyptian 140, 141
  Spiny 140, 142
Mealworms as food 45
Mineral supplements 48
Mites 65
Monitors 211ff
  Bosc's (or rock) 211
Mountain horned lizard 150

Natural vivaria 32ff
Naultinus species 108
  elegans 107
Nephrurus species 91
  laevissimus 92
Night lizards 112ff
  desert 112, 113
  granite 112, 113

Oedura species 105
  castelnaui 105, 106
Ophisaurus species 188
  apodus 189
  attenuatus 190
  ventralis 189, 190
Outdoor enclosures 27ff

Pachydactylus species 87
  bibronii 87
Palmatagecko rangei 93, *93*
Parasites, external 65
  internal 66
Parthenogenetic reproduction 175, 183
Petrosaurus species 132
  mearnsi 136
  thalassinus 134
Phelsuma species 94ff
  cepediana 100
  dubia 100
  laticauda 98, *99*
  lineatus 99, 100
  madagascariensis 100
  standingi 100
  sundbergi 100
Phosphorus 49
Phrynocephalus species 138
Phrynosoma species 136
  douglassii 135, 137
  modestum 135
Physignathus species 146
  cocincinus 146, *147*
  lesueurii 148, *149*
Planting, in natural vivaria 32ff
  in outdoor enclosures 29ff
Plated lizards 191ff
  giant (or tawny) 193, *196*
  rough-scaled 193, *196*
Platysaurus species 191, 193
  guttatus 195
Podarcis species 171, 173
  lilfordi 176
  lilfordi lilfordi 178
  muralis 174, 176
  muralis brueggmanni 176
  pityusensis 175, 176
  pityusensis vedrae 176
  sicula 176
Pogona species 142
  barbatus 146
  vitticeps 142, 143, *143*, *145*
Pre-anal pores 53
Protozoan infection 67
Psammodromus species 173
  algirus 177, 178
  hispanicus 178
Pseudocordylus species 191, 193
  microlepidotus 193
Ptychozoon species 84
  kuhli 83, 84
Pygopods 110ff
Pygopus species 111
  lepidopodus 111

Racerunners 181
  six-lined 182
Rainbow lizard (Agamidae) 148, 152

Rainbow lizard (Teiidae) 182
Rhacodactylus species 109
  auriculatus 107, 109
  chahoua 109
  trachyrhynchus 109
Riopa species 165
Rock lizards (Cordylidae) 191
Rock lizards (Iguanidae) 132
  banded 136
  Baja blue 134
Rock lizards (Lacertidae)
  Caucasian 175
Ruin lizard 176

Salmonella infections 68
Sandfish 168
Sauromalus species 114, 118
  hispidus 119
  obesus 118, *119*
Sceloporus species 114, 128
  jarrovii 128
  malachitus 128
  occidentalis 128
  orcutti 128
Scincidae 154ff
Scincus scincus 168
Sexing 52ff
Shinisaurus crocodilurus 168, 203, *203*
Short-horned lizard *135*, 137
Side-blotched lizard 129, *129*
Skinks 154ff
  Berber 169, *170*
  Blue-tongued 155ff
    blotched *155* 156
    central 156
    eastern 155
    New Guinea 156, *156*
    western 155
  broad-headed 164, *166*
  Cunningham's 161
  eyed 169
  five-lined *167*
  monkey-tailed 160, *162*
  pink-tongued 155, 156, 158
  prehensile-tailed 160, *162*
  Solomon Island 160, 162
  stump-tailed 155, 157, *157*
Slow-worm 189, 190
Snake lizards (Cordylidae) 191ff
Snake lizards (Pygopodidae) 110ff
  Burton's 110
Sphaerodactyline geckos 102ff
Sphaerodactylus species 104
  cinereus 104, *104*
Spiny lizards 114
  granite 128
  malachite 128
Spiny-footed lizard 173, *173*
Spiny-tailed iguanas 114

Stenodactylus 35
Striped gonatodes *103*, 105
Swifts 114
    Chilean 114, 130, *130*, *131*
    Yarrow's 128
Sungazer 191
Supplements (food) 48ff

Takydromus species 173
    sexlineatus 178, *178*
Tarentola mauretanica 84, *85*
Tebos as food 46
Tegus 181, 183
    common *183*
Teiidae 181ff
Teius species 181
Temperature (general) 13
Temperature dependent sex determination
    (TDSD) 16, 57
Teratoscincus species *94*
    microlepis 93
    przewalksii 93
    scincus 93
Tetradactylus species 191, 196
Territories 14, 54
Thermoregulation 13
Ticks 65
Tiliqua species 154ff
    gerrardii 155, 156, 158, 160
    gigas 155, 156, *156*, 160
    multifasciata 156, 160
    nigrolutea 155, 156, 159, 160
    occipitalis 155, 160
    rugosus 155, 157, *157*, 160
    scincoides 155, 159, 160
Tokay *58*, 83
Tracheloptychus species 195
Trachydosaurus rugosus see *Tiliqua rugosus*
Tree lizards 129
Trogonophis weigmanni 215
Tropidophorus species 165
    grayi 168
'Trulite' 24
Tupinambis species 181
    rufescens 181
    teguixin 181, *181*

Ultra-violet lighting 24ff
Uma species 132, 134
Uromastyx species 138
    acanthinurus 140, *142*
    aegypticus 140, *141*
    hardwickii 140
Urosaurus species 129
Uta stansburiana 129, *129*

'Vapona' 66
Varanus species 211ff
    exanthematicus 211, 212
    komodoensis 212
    niloticus 212
    prasinus 212
    salvator 212
Vitamin D 15ff, 24, 50
    deficiency 65
Vitamin supplements 48ff
Viviparous lizard *174*

Wall lizards 171ff
    common *174*, 176
    Ibiza *175*, 176
    Lilford's 176
    Vedra 176
Water dragons 146
    Asian (Thai) 146, *147*
    eastern 148, *149*
Waxworms as food 45
Whiptails 181
    Chihuahuan 183
    desert grassland *182*, 183
    western 182
Worm lizards 214ff
Worms (parasitic) 66

Xantusia henshawi 112, *113*
    vigilis 112, *113*
Xantusiidae 112ff

Zebra-tailed lizard 132, *133*, 134
Zonosaurus species 195

Keeping
and
Breeding
Lizards